The 2023 Ul
Air Fryer Cookb⌐⌐⌐

1000 Days of Easy, Delicious, Budget-Friendly and Foolproof Air Fryer Recipes For Everyday Air Frying For The Family And Friends.

Rosalee Larson

Table of Contents

Introduction

As Air Fryers has been introduced to the UK market, the demand for healthy, delicious and safe recipes has never been so high. THE UK AIR FRYER COOKBOOK is designed to give you an extensive collection of air fryer recipes tailored to the UK market. From breaded fish to cheese burgers and delicious fries, you will be able to cook a range of great and healthy recipes.

Each recipe is followed by the necessary cooking instructions, ingredients, instructions and tips in order to ensure that you cook the recipe in your air fryer as suitable.

The air fryer is a wonderful gadget which can cook tasty and healthy meals by eliminating the need for oil. The air fryers uses minimal oil but still produces amazing crispy food. You also need to know that not all recipes will work with all air fryers. This cookbook will benefit you in having a great collection of recipes that you can use at your home. In this cookbook, there are easy to follow instructions and recipes that you can use for your family at the same time. A lot of people already love air fryers because of their convenience and the fact that they are healthy. With this cookbook, you will be able to use your air fryer even more than before. You will be able to cook more healthy meals with your air fryer. This cookbook will guide you in choosing the right air fryer which is great for cooking. There are easy to follow recipes that can be made with the air fryer. With this book, you will be able to make your own healthy meals that won't leave you feeling bloated. This book is well worth it and will help you save money by cooking at home. It is a must have for all air fryers and will help everyone in the kitchen. This cookbook will help you in getting the most out of your air fryer and to be able to use it for cooking.

Lastly, I hope that you will enjoy making and eating the recipes in this book and that they will bring happiness and joy to your kitchen and your life.

Let's get air frying!

Air fryer Essential Accessories

Your air fryer's cooking chamber is basically just a large, open space for the hot air to circulate. This is a huge advantage because it gives you the option to incorporate several different accessories into your cooking. These accessories broaden the number of recipes you can make in your air fryer and open up options you never would've thought were possible. Here are some of the common accessories.

Metal holder. This circular rack is used to add a second layer to your cooking surface so you can maximize space and cook multiple things at once. It's particularly helpful when you're cooking meat and vegetables and don't want to wait for one to finish to get started on the other.

Skewer rack. Similar to a metal holder, it has built-in metal skewers that make roasting kebabs a breeze.

Ramekins. Small 4" ramekins are great for making mini cakes and quiches. If they're oven safe, they're safe to use in your air fryer.

Cake pans. You can find specially made cake pans for your air fryer that fit perfectly into the cooking chamber. They also come with a built-in handle so you can easily pull them out when your cakes are done baking.

Cupcake pan. A cupcake pan usually comes with seven mini cups and takes up the entire chamber of a 5.3-quart air fryer. These versatile cups are perfect for muffins, cupcakes, and even eggs. If you don't want to go this route, you can also use individual silicone baking cups or aluminum cups.

Parchment paper. Any parchment paper will work in the air fryer, but there are some ways to make this step even easier. Specially precut parchment can make cleanup even easier when baking with your air fryer. Additionally, you can find parchment paper with precut holes for easy steaming. Cooking spray. Although the air fryer cooks with little to no oil, there are some cases in which a little spray is essential. Especially in recipes that involve breading and flour, like fried chicken, spritzing oil on the outside helps you get a brown and crispy exterior for a much tastier end product.

Accessory Removal

Some pans can be more difficult to remove than others because of their size and the depth of the fryer basket. Here are some tools that will allow you to take items out of your appliance safely and easily.

Tongs. These will be helpful when lifting meat in and out of the air fryer. Tongs are also useful for removing cooking pans that don't come with handles.

Oven mitts. Sometimes simple is best. Your food will be very hot when you remove it, so it's great to have these around to protect your hands. Traditional oven mitts or even silicone mitts are great options.

Cleaning Your Air Fryer

Before cleaning it, first ensure that your air fryer is completely cool and unplugged. To clean the air fryer pan you'll need to:

Remove the air fryer pan from the base. Fill the pan with hot water and dish soap. Let the pan soak with the frying basket inside for 10 minutes.

Clean the basket thoroughly with a sponge or brush.

Remove the fryer basket and scrub the underside and outside walls.

Clean the air fryer pan with a sponge or brush.

Let everything air-dry and return to the air fryer base.

To clean the outside of your air fryer, simply wipe with a damp cloth. Then, be sure all components are in the correct position before beginning your next cooking adventure.

Tips For Using Your New Air Fryer

If you are a beginner with an air fryer, here are a few tips for using your new appliance to help you get the best results:

Preheat your air fryer for optimal results- Preheating your air fryer for 3 to 5 minutes is a good practice to get the best out of your ingredients. It saves you time during the cooking process, and the taste and the look of your food will be better!

Avoid the smoke while cooking- Fatty food such as bacon, meatballs, lard, etc., can emit a lot of smoke while being cooked in an air fryer. You can add a bit of water under the air fryer basket to combat this. With this intelligent method, you kill two birds with one stone because you will also get the succulent taste of the meal and create the delicious gravy.

Grease the air fryer basket- Greasing your air fryer basket with a little oil is the secret to avoiding food sticking to the basket, which is a very annoying problem. This advice is highly recommended for lean foods that will release little fat during the cooking process.

Do not overload your air fryer- Your food is cooked by the air circulating in the basket, so it is essential not to overload your air fryer. Keeping room inside your air fryer basket will ensure you get a crispy and browned crust on most foods, so keep that in mind.

Shake helps to cook better- At the middle of the cooking cycle, shake the ingredients a little in the air fryer. As a result, your food will be perfectly cooked on each side.

Put enough space for large ingredients- It is better to space them out so that they do not overlap each other and you can still place a few small items in your air fryer at a time. This will help to keep heat distribution even and prevent food from burning on the outside while being raw on the inside. Also, make sure that you have more space around the air filter so that it can breathe freely.

Use a parchment paper when cooking messy ingredients- If you are cooking something messy like eggs, potatoes, etc., use parchment paper to avoid the mess from dripping in the air fryer. This will help to prevent the food from sticking to the basket and making it hard to remove from the machine. Just make sure that you remove the parchment when the food is completely cooked.

Sprinkle your food with oil before cooking it- Using oil spray on your food is the best way to make your food crispier and tastier.

Use bread slices to soak extra grease- If you don't have a foil to collect the extra grease at home, then you can solve the problem with bread; placing a slice of bread at the bottom of your air fryer is an easy way to catch extra grease and drips.

Never clean the air fryer in the dishwasher- An air fryer can be cleaned with regular water and detergent by disassembling the various components. Washing an air fryer in the dishwasher can damage it, so please be careful about that.

FAQs

Do you need to use oil with the air fryer?

You just have to spray a bit of oil so the food doesn't get stuck in the air fryer basket, and food gets that golden brown color you want.

What should I avoid cooking in the air fryer?

Do not cook foods that require water, such as grains and rice. If you are using batter, freeze the battered food first to make it hard. Then bake in the air fryer.

Why do I have to shake the air fryer basket?

You need to shake the air fryer basket or flip the food for even cooking.

Why don't some types of foods turn out crispy?

Usually, vegetables will not get a crunchy outer layer.

Coating food items with bread crumbs will give them an extra crunch.

Do not overcrowd the cooking basket. It will prevent crunchiness.

Can I steam in the air fryer?

No, you can't steam foods in the air fryer. You need to heat the water from below to steam, but the air fryer heats the food from above.

Why do I have overcooked or burned food?

Check your food several times during the cooking process to prevent this from happening.

If you cook food in batches, you need to check the second batch of foods earlier because the air fryer will already be hot and will cook the second and third batches of food faster.

Do I need to preheat the air fryer?

Preheating can help you cut down on cooking time.

How do I prevent foods from getting stuck to the air fryer basket?

You need to spray a bit of oil on your food to prevent sticking. Using parchment paper also helps.

How do I safely remove foods from the air fryer?

Finish cooking, then remove the air fryer basket from the air fryer.

Use a pair of tongs to remove food safely from the basket.

Can I cook different foods in the air fryer?

Yes, you can cook different foods in your air fryer. You can use it for cooking different types of foods like casseroles and even desserts.

How much food can I put inside?

Different air fryers have different capacities. To know how much food, you can put in, look for the "Max" mark and use it as a guide to filling the basket.

Can I add extra ingredients during the cooking process?

Yes, you can. Just open the air fryer and add ingredients. There is no need to change the internal temperature to stabilize once you close the air fryer chamber.

Can I put aluminum or baking paper at the bottom of the air fryer?

Yes, you can use either to line the base of the air fryer. However, make sure that you poke holes so that the hot air can pass through the material and cook food properly.

Why does it take the food more time to cook?

Your pieces of meat or vegetables are larger than the recipe calls for.

You are using a deeper cake pan than specified.

You are doubling the recipe.

Why is the food only partly cooked?

You need to cook food in one layer in batches.

CHAPTER 1: Breakfast

1. Egg in a Hole

Preparation Time: 5 minutes

Cooking time: 5 minutes

Servings: 1

Ingredients:

- 1 slice bread
- 15g butter, softened
- 1 egg
- Salt and pepper, to taste
- 15g shredded Cheddar cheese
- 15g diced ham

Directions:

1. Preheat the air fryer to 166ºC. Place a baking dish in the air fryer basket. On a flat work surface, cut a hole in the center of the bread slice with a 2½-inch-diameter biscuit cutter.
2. Spread the butter evenly on each side of the bread slice and transfer it to the baking dish.
3. Crack the egg into the hole then season as desired with salt and pepper. Scatter the shredded cheese and diced ham on top.
4. Bake in the preheated air fryer for 5 minutes until the bread is lightly browned and the egg is cooked to your preference. Remove from the basket and serve hot.

Nutrition: Calories: 172kcal; Carbs: 16g; Fat: 8g; Protein: 8g

2. Blueberry Cobbler

Preparation Time: 5 minutes

Cooking time: 15 minutes

Servings: 4

Ingredients:

- 3.7g baking powder
- 80g whole-wheat pastry flour
- Dash sea salt
- 80g unsweetened nondairy milk
- 28.3g maple syrup
- 2.84g vanilla
- Cooking spray
- 100g blueberries
- 50g granola
- Nondairy yogurt, for topping (optional)

Directions:

1. Preheat the fryer to 175ºC. Spritz a baking pan with cooking spray.
2. Mix the baking powder, flour, plus salt in a medium bowl. Put the milk, maple syrup, plus vanilla and whisk to combine.
3. Scrape the mixture into the prepared pan. Scatter the blueberries and granola on top.
4. Transfer the pan to your air fryer and bake for 15 minutes, or until the top begins to brown and a knife inserted in the center comes out clean.
5. Let the cobbler cool for 5 minutes and serve with a drizzle of nondairy yogurt.

Nutrition: Calories: 279kcal; Carbs: 56g; Fat: 5g; Protein: 3g

3. Peppered Maple Bacon Knots

Preparation Time: 5 minutes

Cooking time: 7-8 minutes

Servings: 6

Ingredients:

- 450g maple smoked center-cut bacon
- 50ml maple syrup

- 50g brown sugar
- Coarsely cracked black peppercorns, to taste

Directions:
1. Warm the air fryer to 199ºC. On a clean work surface, tie each bacon strip in a loose knot.
2. Stir together the maple syrup and brown sugar in a bowl. Generously brush this mixture over the bacon knots.
3. Working in batches, arrange the bacon knots in the air fryer basket. Sprinkle with the coarsely cracked black peppercorns.
4. Air fry for 5 minutes. Flip the bacon knots and continue cooking for 2 to 3 minutes more, or until the bacon is crisp.
5. Remove from the basket to a paper towel-lined plate. Repeat with the remaining bacon knots. Let the bacon knots cool for a few minutes and serve warm.

Nutrition: Calories: 110kcal; Carbs: 0g; Fat: 9g; Protein: 7g

4. Turkey Breakfast Sausage Patties

Preparation Time: 5 minutes

Cooking time: 10 minutes

Servings: 4

Ingredients:

- 15g chopped fresh thyme
- 15g chopped fresh sage
- 16.42g kosher salt
- 5g chopped fennel seeds
- 3.7g smoked paprika
- 2.84g onion powder
- 2.84g garlic powder
- 1g crushed red pepper flakes – 1 g freshly ground black pepper
- 450g 93% lean ground turkey
- 100g finely minced sweet apple (peeled)

Directions:

1. Combine the thyme, sage, salt, fennel seeds, paprika, onion powder, garlic powder, red pepper flakes, plus black pepper in a medium bowl.
2. Put the ground turkey and apple and stir well. Divide the batter into eight equal portions then shape into patties with your hands, each about ¼ inch thick and 3 inches in diameter.
3. Warm the air fryer to 204ºC. Place the patties in the air fryer basket in a single layer.
4. Air fry for 5 minutes. Flip the patties and air fry for 5 minutes, or until the patties are nicely browned and cooked through.

5. Remove from the basket to a plate and repeat with the remaining patties. Serve warm.

Nutrition: Calories: 110kcal; Carbs: 0g; Fat: 5g; Protein: 16g

5. Glazed Strawberry Toast

Preparation Time: 5 minutes

Cooking time: 8 minutes

Servings: 4 toasts

Ingredients:

- 4 slices of bread, ½-inch thick
- 250 g sliced strawberries

- 5g sugar
- Cooking spray

Directions:

1. Warm the air fryer to 191ºC. On a clean work surface, lay the bread slices and spritz one side of each slice of bread with cooking spray.
2. Put the bread slices in your air fryer basket, sprayed side down. Top with the strawberries and a sprinkle of sugar.
3. Air fry for 8 minutes until the toast is well browned on each side. Remove from the air fryer basket to a plate and serve.

Nutrition: Calories: 261kcal; Carbs: 48g; Fat: 7g; Protein: 2g

6. Cinnamon Sweet Potato Chips

Preparation Time: 5 minutes

Cooking time: 8 minutes

Servings: 6-8

Ingredients:

- 1 small sweet potato, cut into 3/8-inch-thick slices
- 28.3ml olive oil
- 5g to 10g ground cinnamon

Directions:

1. Warm the air fryer to 199ºC. Add the sweet potato slices and olive oil in a bowl and toss to coat. Fold in the cinnamon and stir to combine.
2. Arrange your sweet potato slices in a single layer in the air fryer basket. Air fry for 8 minutes, or until the chips are crisp. Shake the basket halfway through.
3. Remove from the air fryer basket and allow to cool for 5 minutes before serving.

Nutrition: Calories: 150kcal; Carbs: 18g; Fat: 7g; Protein: 1g

7. 5- Ingredient Vanilla Granola

Preparation Time: 5 minutes

Cooking time: 40 minutes

Servings: 4

Ingredients:

- 250g rolled oats
- 42.52g maple syrup
- 15g sunflower oil
- 15g coconut sugar

- 1.42g vanilla
- 1.42g cinnamon
- 1.42g sea salt

Directions:

1. Preheat the air fryer to 120ºC. Mix together the oats, maple syrup, sunflower oil, coconut sugar, vanilla, cinnamon, and sea salt in a medium bowl and stir to combine. Transfer the mixture to a baking pan.
2. Put your pan in the air fryer basket and bake for 40 minutes, or until the granola is mostly dry and lightly browned. Stir the granola four times during cooking.
3. Let the granola stand for 5 to 10 minutes before serving.

Nutrition: Calories: 205kcal, Carbs: 37g, Fat: 7g, Protein: 4g

8. Eggs in Bell Pepper Rings

Preparation Time: 5 minutes

Cooking time: 10-16 minutes

Servings: 4

Ingredients:

- 1 large red, yellow/orange bell pepper, cut into four ¾-inch rings
- 4 eggs
- Salt, to taste
- freshly ground black pepper, to taste
- 8.4g salsa
- Cooking spray

Directions:

1. Warm the air fryer to 177ºC. Coat a baking pan lightly with cooking spray.
2. Put 2 bell pepper rings in the prepared baking pan. Crack one egg into each bell pepper ring and sprinkle with salt and pepper. Top each egg with 2.84g of salsa.
3. Put the baking pan in your air fryer basket and air fry for 5 to 8 minutes, or until the eggs are cooked to your desired doneness.
4. Remove from the pan to a plate and repeat with the remaining bell pepper rings, eggs, and salsa. Serve warm.

Nutrition: Calories: 150kcal, Carbs: 3g, Fat: 9g, Protein: 13g

9. Easy Buttermilk Biscuits

Preparation Time: 5 minutes

Cooking time: 18 minutes

Servings: 16 biscuits

Ingredients:

- 600g all-purpose flour
- 15g baking powder
- 5g kosher salt
- 5g sugar
- 2.84g baking soda
- 70g (1 stick) unsalted butter, at room temperature
- 250g buttermilk, chilled

Directions:

1. Stir together the flour, baking powder, salt, sugar, and baking powder in a large bowl. Add the butter and stir to mix well. Pour in the buttermilk and stir with a rubber spatula just until incorporated.
2. Put your dough onto a lightly floured surface and roll the dough out to a disk, ½ inch thick. Cut out the biscuits with a 2-inch round cutter and re-roll any scraps until you have 16 biscuits.
3. Preheat the air fryer to 163ºC. Working in batches, arrange the biscuits in the air fryer basket in a single layer.
4. Bake within 18 minutes until the biscuits are golden brown. Remove then repeat with the remaining biscuits. Serve hot.

Nutrition: Calories: 150kcal, Carbs: 30g, Fat: 2g, Protein: 4g

10. Bourbon Vanilla French Toast

Preparation Time: 15 minutes

Cooking time: 6 minutes

Servings: 4

Ingredients:

- 2 large eggs
- 28.3ml water
- 150g whole or 2% milk
- 15g butter, melted
- 28.3g bourbon
- 5g vanilla extract
- 8 (1-inch-thick) French bread slices
- Cooking spray

Directions:

1. Warm the air fryer to 160ºC. Prepare the air fryer basket using parchment paper and spray it with cooking spray.

2. Beat the eggs plus the water in a shallow bowl until combined. Add the milk, melted butter, bourbon, and vanilla and stir to mix well.

3. Dredge 4 slices of bread in the batter, turning to coat both sides evenly. Transfer the bread slices onto the parchment paper.

4. Bake for 6 minutes until nicely browned. Flip your slices halfway through the cooking time. Remove then repeat with the remaining 4 slices of bread. Serve warm.

Nutrition: Calories: 330kcal, Carbs: 44g, Fat: 8g, Protein: 0g

11. Herbed Cheddar Frittata

Preparation Time: 10 minutes

Cooking time: 20 minutes

Servings: 4

Ingredients:

- 120 g shredded Cheddar cheese
- 120g half-and-half
- 4 large eggs
- 30g chopped scallion greens
- 30g chopped fresh parsley
- 2.84g kosher salt
- 2.84g ground black pepper
- Cooking spray

Directions:

1. Warm the air fryer to 149ºC. Spritz a baking pan with cooking spray. Whisk together all the fixings in a large bowl, then pour the mixture into the prepared baking pan.

2. Set the pan in the preheated air fryer and bake for 20 minutes or until set. Serve immediately.

Nutrition: Calories: 180kcal, Carbs: 18g, Fat: 7g, Protein: 13g

12. Kale Frittata

Preparation Time: 5 minutes

Cooking time: 11 minutes

Servings: 2

Ingredients:

- 250g kale, chopped
- 5ml olive oil
- 4 large eggs, beaten
- Kosher salt, to taste

- 28.3ml water
- 42.52g crumbled feta
- Cooking spray

Directions:

1. Warm the air fryer to 182ºC. Spritz an air fryer baking pan with cooking spray. Add the kale to the baking pan and drizzle with olive oil. Arrange the pan in the preheated air fryer. Broil for 3 minutes.
2. Meanwhile, combine the eggs with salt and water in a large bowl. Stir to mix well. Make the frittata: When the broiling time is complete, pour the eggs into the baking pan and spread with feta cheese. Adjust the temperature to 149ºC.
3. Bake for 8 minutes or until the eggs are set and the cheese melts. Remove then serve the frittata immediately.

Nutrition: Calories: 195kcal, Carbs: 5g, Fat: 14g, Protein: 14g

13. Sausage and Cheese Quiche

Preparation Time: 5 minutes

Cooking time: 25 minutes

Servings: 4

Ingredients:

- 12 large eggs
- 250g heavy cream
- Salt and black pepper, to taste
- 340g sugar-free breakfast sausage
- 400g shredded Cheddar cheese
- Cooking spray

Directions:

1. Warm the air fryer to 191ºC. Coat a casserole dish with cooking spray.
2. Beat together the eggs, heavy cream, salt and pepper in a large bowl until creamy. Stir in the breakfast sausage and Cheddar cheese.
3. Pour the sausage mixture into the prepared casserole dish and bake for 25 minutes, or until the top of the quiche is golden brown and the eggs are set.
4. Remove from the air fryer then let sit for 5 to 10 minutes before serving.

Nutrition: Calories: 493kcal, Carbs: 23g, Fat: 34g, Protein: 21g

14. Cheesy Breakfast Casserole

Preparation Time: 10 minutes

Cooking time: 14 minutes

Servings: 4

Ingredients:

- 6 slices bacon
- 6 eggs
- Salt and pepper, to taste
- Cooking spray
- 120g chopped green bell pepper
- 120g chopped onion
- 150g shredded Cheddar cheese

Directions:

1. Put the bacon in your skillet over medium-high heat and cook each side for about 4 minutes until evenly crisp. Remove from the heat to a paper towel-lined plate to drain. Crumble it into small pieces and set it aside.
2. Whisk the eggs with salt and pepper in a medium bowl. Warm the air fryer to 204ºC. Spritz a baking pan with cooking spray.
3. Place the whisked eggs, crumbled bacon, green bell pepper, and onion in the prepared pan. Bake in the preheated air fryer for 6 minutes.
4. Scatter the Cheddar cheese all over and bake for 2 minutes more. Allow to sit within 5 minutes and serve on plates.

Nutrition: Calories: 358kcal, Carbs: 0g, Fat: 22g, Protein: 0g

15. Western Omelet

Preparation Time: 5 minutes

Cooking time: 18-21 minutes

Servings: 2

Ingredients:

- 50g chopped bell pepper, green or red – 50 g cup chopped onion
- 50g diced ham
- 4 large eggs
- 30 ml milk
- 1/8 teaspoon salt
- 150g shredded sharp Cheddar cheese

Directions:

1. Warm the air fryer to 199ºC. Put the bell pepper, onion, ham, and butter in a baking pan and mix well.
2. Air fry within 1 minute. Stir and continue to air fry again within 4 to 5 minutes until the veggies are softened. Meanwhile, whisk together the eggs, milk, and salt in a bowl.

3. Pour the egg batter over the veggie batter. Reduce the air fryer temperature to 182ºC and bake for 13 to 15 minutes more, or until the top is lightly golden browned and the eggs are set.

4. Scatter the omelet with the shredded cheese. Bake for another 1 minute until the cheese has melted. Let the omelet cool within 5 minutes before serving.

Nutrition: Calories: 290kcal, Carbs: 12g, Fat: 18g, Protein: 22g

16.Cornmeal Pancake

Preparation Time: 10 minutes

Cooking time: 10-12 minutes

Servings: 4

Ingredients:

- 350g yellow cornmeal
- 120g all-purpose flour
- 28.3g sugar
- 5g salt
- 5g baking powder
- 250 ml whole or 2% milk
- 1 large egg, lightly beaten
- 15g butter, melted
- Cooking spray

Directions:

1. Warm the air fryer to 177ºC. Prepare the air fryer basket with parchment paper.

2. Stir together the cornmeal, flour, sugar, salt, and baking powder in a large bowl. Mix in the milk, egg, and melted butter and whisk to combine.

3. Working in batches, drop tablespoonfuls of the batter onto the parchment paper for each pancake.

4. Spray the pancakes with cooking spray and bake for 3 minutes. Flip the pancakes, spray with cooking spray again, and bake for an additional 2 to 3 minutes.

5. Remove then repeat with the remaining batter. Cool for 5 minutes and serve immediately.

Nutrition: Calories: 72kcal, Carbs: 15g, Fat: 3g, Protein: 3g

17.Fried Cheese Grits

Preparation Time: 10 minutes

Cooking time: 10-12 minutes

Servings: 4

Ingredients:

- 150g instant grits

- 5g salt
- 5g freshly ground black pepper
- 150ml whole or 2% milk
- 90g cream cheese, at room temperature
- 1 large egg, beaten
- 15g butter, melted
- 250g shredded mild Cheddar cheese
- Cooking spray

Directions:

1. Mix the grits, salt, and black pepper in a large bowl. Add the milk, cream cheese, beaten egg, and melted butter and whisk to combine. Fold in the Cheddar cheese and stir well.
2. Warm the air fryer to 204ºC. Spray a baking pan with cooking spray. Spread the grits mixture into the baking pan and place it in the air fryer basket.
3. Air fry for 10 to 12 minutes, or until the grits are cooked and a knife inserted in the center comes out clean. Stir the batter once halfway through the cooking time.
4. Rest for 5 minutes and serve warm.

Nutrition: Calories: 282kcal, Carbs: 26g, Fat: 14g, Protein: 13g

18. Veggie Frittata

Preparation Time: 10 minutes

Cooking time: 8-12 minutes

Servings: 4

Ingredients:

- 120g chopped red bell pepper
- 80g grated carrot
- 80g minced onion
- 5ml olive oil
- 1 egg
- 6 egg whites – 80 ml 2% milk
- 15g shredded Parmesan cheese

Directions:

1. Warm the air fryer to 177ºC. Mix together the red bell pepper, carrot, onion, and olive oil in a baking pan and stir to combine.
2. Transfer the pan to your air fryer and bake for 4 to 6 minutes until the veggies are soft. Shake the basket once during cooking.
3. Meantime, whisk together the egg, egg whites, and milk in a medium bowl until creamy. Pour the egg batter over the top of the veggies. Scatter with the Parmesan cheese.

4. Bake within an additional 4 to 6 minutes, or until the eggs are set and the top is golden around the edges. Allow the frittata to cool within 5 minutes before slicing and serving.

Nutrition: Calories: 158kcal, Carbs: 6g, Fat: 9g,Protein: 15g

19.Mixed Berry Dutch Baby Pancake

Preparation Time: 10 minutes

Cooking time: 12-16 minutes

Servings: 4

Ingredients:

- 15g unsalted butter, at room temperature
- 1 egg
- 2 egg whites
- 100ml 2% milk
- 100 g whole-wheat pastry flour
- 5g pure vanilla extract
- 250 g sliced fresh strawberries
- 100 g fresh raspberries
- 100 g fresh blueberries

Directions:

1. Preheat the air fryer to 166ºC. Grease a baking pan with butter. Beat together the egg, egg whites, milk, pastry flour, and vanilla using a hand mixer, in a medium mixing bowl until well incorporated.
2. Pour the batter to the pan and bake in the preheated air fryer for 12 to 16 minutes, or until the pancake puffs up in the center and the edges are golden brown.
3. Allow the pancake to cool for 5 minutes and serve topped with the berries.

Nutrition: Calories: 350kcal, Carbs: 57g, Fat: 7g, Protein: 14g

20. Banana and Oat Bread Pudding

Preparation Time: 10 minutes

Cooking time: 16-20 minutes

Servings: 4

Ingredients:

- 2 medium ripe bananas, mashed
- 100ml low-fat milk
- 28.3g maple syrup
- 28.3g peanut butter
- 5g vanilla extract

- 5g ground cinnamon
- 2 slices whole-grain bread, cut into bite-sized cubes
- 50 g quick oats
- Cooking spray

Directions:

1. Preheat the fryer to 177ºC. Spritz a baking dish lightly with cooking spray.
2. Mix the bananas, milk, maple syrup, peanut butter, vanilla, and cinnamon in a large mixing bowl and stir until well incorporated.
3. Add the bread cubes to the banana mixture and stir until thoroughly coated. Fold in the oats and stir to combine.
4. Transfer the mixture to the baking dish. Wrap the baking dish in aluminum foil. Air fry within 10 to 12 minutes until heated through.
5. Remove the foil and cook for an additional 6 to 8 minutes, or until the pudding has set. Let the pudding cool for 5 minutes before serving.

Nutrition: Calories: 132kcal, Carbs: 21g, Fat: 4g, Protein: 3g

CHAPTER 2: Poultry Recipes

21.Sweet Citrusy Chicken

Preparation Time: 10 minutes

Cooking time: 14 minutes

Servings: 2

Ingredients:

- 600g chicken thighs, boneless and skinless
- 28.3g cornflour
- 60ml orange juice
- 28.3g brown sugar
- 15g soy sauce
- 15g rice wine vinegar
- 1.42g ground ginger

- Pinch of red pepper flakes
- Zest of 1 orange
- 8.4ml water & 8.4g cornflour, mixed

Directions:

1. Preheat your air fryer to 250ºC.
2. Combine the chicken and corn flour in a bowl. Add the chicken in your basket, and cook within 9 minutes. Set aside.
3. Mix the remaining fixings except for the cornflour mixture in your bowl. Pour it in your skillet, boil, and adjust to a simmer within 5 minutes.
4. Pour the cornflour mixture to your skillet, then mix it well. Pour this sweet citrus sauce on top of your chicken and enjoy!

Nutrition: Calories: 546kcal; Carbs: 34g; Fat: 6g; Protein: 2g

22. Tandoori Chicken

Preparation Time: 15 minutes

Cooking time: 15 minutes

Servings: 2

Ingredients:

- 500g chicken tenders, halved
- 15g each of minced ginger& garlic
- 5g cayenne pepper

- 5g turmeric
- 5g garam masala
- 60ml yoghurt
- 25g coriander leaves
- Salt & pepper, as needed

Directions:

1. Add all the ingredients except the chicken in a large bowl. Once combined, add the chicken and toss it well until fully coated.
2. Warm up the air fryer to 160ºC, put the tandoori chicken in your basket and baste it with oil. Cook within 10 minutes, turn it over and cook again within 5 minutes. Serve!

Nutrition: Calories: 178kcal; Carbs: 2g; Fat: 6g; Protein: 25g

23. Chicken Meatballs

Preparation Time: 20 minutes

Cooking time: 9 minutes

Servings: 4

Ingredients:

- 500g minced chicken
- 1 egg
- 15g dried oregano
- 20g garlic paste
- 5g lemon zest

- 5g dried onion powder
- Salt & pepper, as needed

Directions:

1. Mix all the fixings in your large bowl and make the meatballs out of this mixture.
2. Preheat your air fryer to 260ºC. Add the meatballs in one layer to the air fryer basket and cook for 9 minutes. Serve and enjoy!

Nutrition: Calories: 346kcal; Carbs: 34g; Fat: 6g; Protein: 19g

24. Chicken Buffalo Wings

Preparation Time: 10 minutes

Cooking time: 30 minutes

Servings: 2

Ingredients:

- 200g chicken wings
- 35g butter
- 42g hot pepper sauce
- 15g vinegar
- 7ml of olive oil
- 2.84g of garlic powder
- cayenne pepper, as needed

Directions:

1. Warm your air fryer to 180ºC.
2. Add the chicken wings to your large bowl, drizzle it with oil, and toss until well coated. Put the chicken wings in your basket, and cook within 25 minutes.
3. Remove the basket, flip, and cook within 5 more minutes. Transfer to your serving plate.
4. Stir the remaining fixings in your pan over medium heat. Serve the wings with the sauce on top. Enjoy!

Nutrition: Calories: 236kcal; Carbs: 6.3g; Fat: 41.5g; Protein: 20.7g

25. Turkey Mushroom Burgers

Preparation Time: 15 minutes

Cooking time: 10 minutes

Servings: 2

Ingredients:

- 180g mushrooms
- 500g minced turkey
- 15g of your favorite chicken seasoning
- 5g each of garlic powder & onion powder
- Salt & pepper to taste
- Cooking spray
- 5 burger buns

Directions:

1. Process the mushrooms in your food processor, add all the seasonings, and mix it well.
2. Transfer mushroom to a bowl and add the minced turkey. Mix it well and shape it into 5 burger patties.
3. Grease it with cooking spray and put it in your basket. Cook at 160ºC for 10 minutes, flipping it halfway through until browned. Stuffed it between the burger buns and serve!

Nutrition: Calories: 132kcal; Carbs: 25g; Fat: 26g; Protein: 25g

26. Buttermilk Marinated Chicken

Preparation Time: 5 minutes

Cooking time: 10 minutes

Servings: 2

Ingredients:

- 250g chicken thighs, skinless & boneless
- 90ml buttermilk
- 20g tapioca flour
- 1.42g garlic salt
- 1 egg
- 35g all-purpose flour
- 1.42g brown sugar
- 2.84g garlic powder
- 1.42g paprika
- 1.42g onion powder
- 1.42g oregano
- Salt, as needed
- pepper, as needed

Directions:

1. Mix the buttermilk and hot sauce in your bowl.
2. Add the tapioca flour, garlic salt, and black pepper to a plastic bag and shake it well to combine.
3. Meanwhile, stir the egg in your other bowl.
4. Dip the chicken thighs into the buttermilk one at a time, then in the tapioca mixture, egg, and flour.
5. Warm your air fryer to 190ºC.
6. Cook the buttermilk chicken for 10 minutes and enjoy!

Nutrition: Calories: 198kcal; Carbs: 7g; Fat: 8g; Protein: 22g

27. Pepper & Lemon Chicken Wings

Preparation Time: 10 minutes

Cooking time: 26 minutes

Servings: 2

Ingredients:

- 1kg chicken wings
- 1.42g cayenne pepper
- 8.4g lemon pepper seasoning +5g for the sauce
- 42g butter, melted

- 5g honey

Directions:

1. Warm up your air fryer to 260ºC.

2. Combine the lemon pepper seasoning and cayenne in a bowl. Mix in the chicken until coated.

3. Put the wings in your basket and cook within 20 minutes. Turn the temperature up to 300ºC and cook for another 6 minutes.

4. Meanwhile, combine the butter, honey, and the rest of the seasoning in a small bowl. Pour the sauce on the wings, and serve.

Nutrition: Calories: 356kcal; Carbs: 31g; Fat: 6g; Protein: 8g

28. Buffalo Chicken Wontons

Preparation Time: 15 minutes

Cooking time: 3-5 minutes

Servings: 6

Ingredients:

- 200g shredded chicken
- 15g buffalo sauce
- 56g softened cream cheese
- 1 sliced spring onion
- 28.3g blue cheese crumbles
- 12 wonton wrappers

Directions:

1. Warm up your air fryer to 200ºC.

2. Combine the chicken and buffalo sauce in a bowl.

3. Mix the cream cheese in another bowl until smooth. Add the scallion, blue cheese, and seasoned chicken and mix it well.

4. Run a wet finger along each edge of your wonton wrappers, place 15g of the filling into the center and fold the corners together.

5. Transfer it to your air fryer basket in one layer and cook at 200ºC for 3 to 5 minutes until golden brown. Serve and enjoy!

Nutrition: Calories: 463kcal; Carbs: 9.4g; Fat: 34g; Protein: 24g

29. Quick & Easy Chicken Tenders

Preparation Time: 10 minutes

Cooking time: 12 minutes

Servings: 2

Ingredients:

- 4 regular chicken tenders
- 1 egg, beaten
- 15ml olive oil
- 75g dried breadcrumbs

Directions:

1. Warm your air fryer to 175ºC.
2. Place the beaten egg in your bowl.
3. Combine the oil and breadcrumbs in another bowl.
4. Coat the chicken into the egg one at a time, then cover it in the breadcrumb mixture.
5. Cook the tenders within 12 minutes and enjoy!

Nutrition: Calories: 250kcal; Carbs: 9.8g; Fat: 11.4g; Protein: 26.2g

30. Chicken Fried Rice

Preparation Time: 10 minutes

Cooking time: 20 minutes

Servings: 4

Ingredients:

- 400g cooked white rice
- 400g cooked chicken, diced
- 200g frozen peas and carrots
- 85g soy sauce
- 15ml vegetable oil
- 1 diced onion

Directions:

1. Combine the rice, oil, and soy sauce in your bowl. Add the frozen peas, carrots, onion, and chicken. Mix it well.
2. Put the mixture into your pan fitted in your air fryer and cook at 182°C for 20 minutes. Serve!

Nutrition: Calories: 224kcal; Carbs: 7.4g; Fat: 43g; Protein: 21.4g

31. Turkey Cutlets with Mushroom Sauce

Preparation Time: 10 minutes

Cooking time: 11 minutes

Servings: 2

Ingredients:

- 2 turkey cutlets
- 15g butter
- 1 can of cream of mushroom sauce
- 160ml milk
- Salt & pepper to taste

Directions:

1. Preheat the air fryer to 220ºC.
2. Brush the turkey cutlets with butter, salt, and pepper. Put the cutlets to your basket and cook for 11 minutes.
3. Add the mushroom soup and milk to a pan and cook for 10 minutes over medium heat, stirring often.
4. Transfer the cooked turkey cutlets to your plate and top it with the sauce. Serve and enjoy!

Nutrition: Calories: 426kcal; Carbs: 18g; Fat: 21g; Protein: 16g

32. Chicken Schnitzel

Preparation Time: 15 minutes

Cooking time: 6 minutes

Servings: 2

Ingredients:

- 150g chicken thighs, boneless, flattened
- 80g seasoned breadcrumbs
- 2.84g ground black pepper
- Salt, as needed
- 15g flour
- 1 beaten egg
- Cooking spray

Directions:

1. Mix the breadcrumbs, salt, and pepper in your bowl. Place the beaten egg in another bowl and the flour into your third bowl.
2. Dredge your chicken into the flour bowl, then in the egg, then evenly coat it in the breadcrumbs.
3. Put the chicken into your basket and grease it with oil.
4. Warm your air fryer to 190ºC and cook the chicken schnitzel for 6 minutes. Enjoy!

Nutrition: Calories: 234kcal; Carbs: 5.6g; Fat: 21.5g; Protein: 21g

33.   Greek Gyros With Chicken & Rice

Preparation Time: 10 minutes

Cooking time: 25 minutes

Servings: 4

Ingredients:

- 1 lb chicken breasts, cubed
- 85g cream cheese
- 28.3g olive oil
- 5g dried oregano
- 5g ground cumin
- 5g ground cinnamon
- 1.42g ground nutmeg
- Salt and pepper to taste
- 1.42g ground turmeric
- 400g cooked rice
- 200g Tzatziki sauce

Directions:

1. Preheat air fryer to 193 degree C. Put all ingredients in a bowl and mix together until the chicken is coated well.

2. Spread the chicken mixture in the frying basket, then Bake for 10 minutes. Stir the chicken mixture and Bake for an additional 5 minutes. Serve with rice and tzatziki sauce.

Nutrition: Calories: 546kcal; Carbs: 34g; Fat: 6g; Protein: 2g

34. Asian Sweet Chili Chicken

Preparation Time: 10 minutes

Cooking time: 20 minutes

Servings: 4

Ingredients:

- 2 chicken breasts, cut into 1-inch pieces
- 240g cornstarch
- 5g chicken seasoning
- Salt and pepper to taste
- 2 eggs
- 300g sweet chili sauce

Directions:

1. Preheat air fryer to 182 degree C. Mix cornstarch, chicken seasoning, salt and pepper in a large bowl. In another bowl, beat the eggs.
2. Dip the chicken in the cornstarch mixture to coat. Next, dip the chicken into the egg, then return to the cornstarch. Transfer chicken to the air fryer.
3. Lightly spray all of the chicken with cooking oil. Air Fry for 15-16 minutes, shaking the basket once or until golden.
4. Transfer chicken to a serving dish and drizzle with sweet-and-sour sauce. Serve immediately.

Nutrition: Calories: 245kcal; Carbs: 34g; Fat: 6g; Protein: 2g

35. Spring Chicken Salad

Preparation Time: 5 minutes

Cooking time: 20 minutes

Servings: 4

Ingredients:

- 3 chicken breasts, cubed
- 1 small red onion, sliced
- 1 red bell pepper, sliced
- 240g green beans, sliced

- 28.3g ranch salad dressing
- 28.3g lemon juice
- 2.84g dried basil
- 10 oz spring mix

Directions:

1. Preheat air fryer to 204 degree C. Put the chicken, red onion, red bell pepper, and green beans in the frying basket and Roast for 10-13 minutes until the chicken is cooked through.
2. Jiggle the basket at least once while cooking. As the chicken is cooking, combine the ranch dressing, lemon juice, and basil.
3. When the chicken is done, remove it and along with the veggies to a bowl and pour the dressing over. Stir to coat. Serve with spring mix.

Nutrition: Calories: 267kcal; Carbs: 24g; Fat: 6g; Protein: 2g

36. Chicken Skewers

Preparation Time: 10 minutes

Cooking time: 45 minutes

Servings: 4

Ingredients:

- 453g boneless skinless chicken thighs, cut into pieces
- 1 sweet onion, cut into 1-inch pieces
- 1 zucchini, cut into 1-inch pieces
- 1 red bell pepper, cut into 1-inch pieces
- 85ml olive oil
- 5g garlic powder
- 5g shallot powder
- 5g ground cumin
- 2.84g dried oregano
- 2.84g dried thyme
- 85ml lemon juice
- 15g apple cider vinegar
- 12 grape tomatoes

Directions:

1. Combine the olive oil, garlic powder, shallot powder, cumin, oregano, thyme, lemon juice, and vinegar in a bowl; mix well. Alternate skewering the chicken, bell pepper, onion, zucchini, and tomatoes.
2. Once all of the skewers are prepared, place them in a greased baking dish and pour the olive oil marinade over the top. Turn to coat. Cover with plastic wrap and refrigerate.

3. Preheat air fryer to 193 degree C. Remove the skewers from the marinade and arrange them in a single layer on the frying basket.

4. Bake for 25 minutes, rotating once. Let the skewers sit for 5 minutes. Serve and enjoy!

Nutrition: Calories: 321kcal; Carbs: 26g; Fat: 5g; Protein: 3g

37. Chicken Flautas

Preparation Time: 5 minutes

Cooking time: 8 minutes

Servings: 6

Ingredients:

- 85g whipped cream cheese
- 240g shredded cooked chicken
- 85g mild pico de gallo salsa
- 113g shredded Mexican cheese
- 2.84g taco seasoning
- Six 8-inch flour tortillas
- 400g shredded lettuce
- 100g guacamole

Directions:

1. Preheat the air fryer to 187g.

2. In a large basin, mix the cream cheese, chicken, salsa, shredded cheese, and taco seasoning until well combined.

3. Lay the tortillas on a flat surface. Divide the cheese-and-chicken mixture into 6 equal portions; then place the mixture in the center of the tortillas, spreading evenly, leaving about 1 inch from the edge of the tortilla.

4. Spritz air fryer basket with olive oil spray. Roll up the flautas and place them edge side down into the basket. Lightly mist the top of the flautas with olive oil spray.

5. Repeat until the air fryer basket is full. You may need to cook these in batches, depending on the size of your air fryer.

6. Cook for 7 minutes, or until the outer edges are browned.

7. Take out from the air fryer basket and serve warm over a bed of shredded lettuce with guacamole on top.

Nutrition: Calories: 346kcal; Carbs: 34g; Fat: 6g; Protein: 2g

38. Chicken Pigs In Blankets

Preparation Time: 10 minutes

Cooking time: 30 minutes

Servings: 4

Ingredients:

- 8 chicken drumsticks, boneless, skinless
- 28.3g light brown sugar
- 28.3g ketchup
- 15g grainy mustard
- 8 smoked bacon slices
- 5g chopped fresh sage

Directions:

1. Preheat the air fryer to 176g. Mix brown sugar, sage, ketchup, and mustard in a bowl and brush the chicken with it.

2. Wrap slices of bacon around the drumsticks and brush with the remaining mix. Line the frying basket with round parchment paper with holes. Set 4 drumsticks on the paper, add a raised rack and set the other drumsticks on it.

3. Bake for 25-35 minutes, moving the bottom drumsticks to the top, top to the bottom, and flipping at about 14-16 minutes. Sprinkle with sage and serve.

Nutrition: Calories: 278kcal; Carbs: 18g; Fat: 7g; Protein: 2g

39. Glazed Chicken Thighs

Preparation Time: 5 minutes

Cooking time: 20 minutes

Servings: 4

Ingredients:

- 453g boneless, skinless chicken thighs
- 85g balsamic vinegar
- 42g honey
- 28.3g brown sugar
- 5g whole-grain mustard
- 85g soy sauce
- 3 garlic cloves, minced
- Salt and pepper to taste
- 2.84g smoked paprika
- 28.3g chopped shallots

Directions:

1. Preheat air fryer to 190g. Whisk vinegar, honey, sugar, soy sauce, mustard, garlic, salt, pepper, and paprika in a small bowl.

2. Arrange the chicken in the frying basket and brush the top of each with some of the vinegar mixture.

3. Air Fry for 7 minutes, then flip the chicken. Brush the tops with the rest of the vinegar mixture and Air Fry for another 5 to 8 minutes.

4. Allow resting for 5 minutes before slicing. Serve warm sprinkled with shallots.

Nutrition: Calories: 299kcal; Carbs: 20g; Fat: 6g; Protein: 5g

40. Italian Herb Stuffed Chicken

Preparation Time: 10 minutes

Cooking time: 20 minutes

Servings: 4

Ingredients:

- 28.3ml olive oil
- 42g balsamic vinegar
- 3 garlic cloves, minced
- 1 tomato, diced
- 28.3g Italian seasoning
- 15g chopped fresh basil
- 5g thyme, chopped
- 4 chicken breasts

Directions:

1. Preheat air fryer to 187 degree C. Combine the olive oil, balsamic vinegar, garlic, thyme, tomato, half of the Italian seasoning, and basil in a medium bowl. Set aside.

2. Cut 4-5 slits into the chicken breasts ¾ of the way through. Season with the rest of the Italian seasoning and place the chicken with the slits facing up, in the greased frying basket.

3. Bake for 7 minutes. Spoon the bruschetta mixture into the slits of the chicken. Cook for another 3 minutes.

4. Allow chicken to sit and cool for a few minutes. Serve and enjoy!

Nutrition: Calories: 546kcal; Carbs: 34g; Fat: 6g; Protein: 2g

CHAPTER 3: Beef, Pork & Lamb Recipes

41.Barbecue-style Beef Cube Steak

Preparation Time: 5 minutes

Cooking time: 14 minutes

Servings: 2

Ingredients:

- 2 4-ounce beef cube steak(s)
- 400g (about 8 ounces) Fritos (original flavor) or a generic corn chip equivalent, crushed to crumbs (see here)
- 85g Purchased smooth barbecue sauce, any flavor (gluten-free, if a concern)

Directions:

1. Preheat the air fryer to 190 degree C.
2. Spread the Fritos crumbs in a shallow soup plate or a small pie plate. Rub the barbecue sauce onto both sides of the steak(s).
3. Dredge the steak(s) in the Fritos crumbs to coat well and thoroughly, turning several times and pressing down to get the little bits to adhere to the meat.
4. When the machine is at temperature, set the steak(s) in the basket. Leave as much air space between them as possible if you're working with more than one piece of beef. Air-fry undisturbed for 12

minutes, or until lightly brown and crunchy. If the air fryer is at 182 degree C, you may need to add 2 minutes to the cooking time.

5. Use kitchen tongs to transfer the steak(s) to a wire rack. Cool for 5 minutes before serving.

Nutrition: Calories: 333kcal; Carbs: 24g; Fat: 6g; Protein: 2g

42. Minted Lamb Chops

Preparation Time: 10 minutes

Cooking time: 20 minutes

Servings: 4

Ingredients:

- 8 lamb chops
- 8.4ml olive oil
- 1 2.84g chopped mint leaves
- 5g ground coriander
- 1 lemon, zested
- 2.84g baharat seasoning
- 1 garlic clove, minced
- Salt and pepper to taste

Directions:

1. Preheat air fryer to 198 degree C. Coat the lamb chops with olive oil. Set aside. Mix mint, coriander, baharat, zest, garlic, salt and pepper in a bowl. Rub the seasoning onto both sides of the chops.

2. Place the chops in the greased frying basket and Air Fry for 10 minutes. Flip the lamb chops and cook for another 5 minutes. Allow the lamb chops rest for a few minutes. Serve right away.

Nutrition: Calories: 289kcal; Carbs: 16g; Fat: 8g; Protein: 2g

43. Tandoori Lamb Samosas

Preparation Time: 10 minutes

Cooking time: 20 minutes

Servings: 2

Ingredients:

- 170g ground lamb, sautéed
- 85g spinach, torn
- ½ onion, minced
- 5g tandoori masala
- 2.84g ginger-garlic paste

- 2.84g red chili powder
- 2.84g turmeric powder
- Salt and pepper to taste
- 3 puff dough sheets

Directions:

1. Preheat air fryer to 176 degree C. Put the ground lamb, tandoori masala, ginger garlic paste, red chili powder, turmeric powder, salt, and pepper in a bowl and stir to combine.

2. Add in the spinach and onion and stir until the ingredients are evenly blended. Divide the mixture into three equal segments.

3. Lay the pastry dough sheets out on a lightly floured surface. Fill each sheet of dough with one of the three portions of lamb mix, then fold the pastry over into a triangle, sealing the edges with a bit of water.

4. Transfer the samosas to the greased frying basket and Air Fry for 12 minutes, flipping once until the samosas are crispy and flaky. Remove and leave to cool for 5 minutes. Serve.

Nutrition: Calories: 546kcal; Carbs: 34g; Fat: 6g; Protein: 2g

44. Classic Beef Meatballs

Preparation Time: 10 minutes

Cooking time: 30 minutes

Servings: 4

Ingredients:

- 42g buttermilk
- 113g bread crumbs
- 15g ketchup
- 1 egg
- 2.84g dried marjoram
- Salt and pepper to taste
- 453g ground beef
- 20 Swiss cheese cubes

Directions:

1. Preheat air fryer to 198 degree C. Mix buttermilk, crumbs, ketchup, egg, marjoram, salt, and pepper in a bowl.

2. Using your hands, mix in ground beef until just combined. Shape into 20 meatballs. Take one meatball and shape it around a Swiss cheese cube. Repeat this for the remaining meatballs.

3. Lightly spray the meatballs with oil and place into the frying basket. Bake the meatballs for 10-13 minutes, turning once until they are cooked through. Serve and enjoy!

Nutrition: Calories: 299kcal; Carbs: 24g; Fat: 6g; Protein: 3g

45. Pork Kabobs With Pineapple

Preparation Time: 5 minutes

Cooking time: 25 minutes

Servings: 4

Ingredients:

- 2 cans juice-packed pineapple chunks, juice reserved
- 1 green bell pepper, cut into ½-inch chunks
- 1 red bell pepper, cut into ½-inch chunks
- 453g pork tenderloin, cubed
- Salt and pepper to taste
- 15g honey
- 2.84g ground ginger
- 2.84g ground coriander
- 1 red chili, minced

Directions:

1. Preheat the air fryer to 190 degree C. Mix the coriander, chili, salt, and pepper in a bowl. Add the pork and toss to coat. Then, thread the pork pieces, pineapple chunks, and bell peppers onto skewers.
2. Combine the pineapple juice, honey, and ginger and mix well. Use all the mixture as you brush it on the kebabs.
3. Put the kebabs in the greased frying basket and Air Fry for 10-14 minutes or until cooked through. Serve and enjoy!

Nutrition: Calories: 301kcal; Carbs: 18g; Fat: 6g; Protein: 2g

46. Apple Cornbread Stuffed Pork Loin With Apple Gravy

Preparation Time: 10 minutes

Cooking time: 50 minutes

Servings: 4

Ingredients:

- 4 strips of bacon, chopped
- One Granny Smith apple, peeled, cored and finely chopped
- 8.4g fresh thyme leaves
- 85g chopped fresh parsley
- 400g cubed cornbread
- 100g chicken stock
- salt and freshly ground black pepper

- 1 (2-pound) boneless pork loin
- kitchen twine

Apple Gravy:

- 28.3g butter
- 1 shallot, minced
- 1 Granny Smith apple, peeled, cored and finely chopped
- 3 sprigs fresh thyme
- 28.3g flour
- 240g chicken stock
- 100g apple cider
- salt and freshly ground black pepper, to taste

Directions:

1. Preheat the air fryer to 204 degree C.
2. Add the bacon to the air fryer and air-fry for 6 minutes until crispy. While the bacon is cooking, combine the apple, fresh thyme, parsley and cornbread in a bowl and toss well.
3. Moisten the mixture with the chicken stock and season to taste with salt and freshly ground black pepper. Add the cooked bacon to the mixture.
4. Butterfly the pork loin by holding it flat on the cutting board with one hand, while slicing into the pork loin parallel to the cutting board with the other.
5. Slice into the longest side of the pork loin, but stop before you cut all the way through. You should then be able to open the pork loin up like a book, making it twice as wide as it was when you started. Season the internal part of the pork with salt and freshly ground black pepper.
6. Spread the cornbread mixture onto the butterflied pork loin, leaving a one-inch border around the edge of the pork. Roll the pork loin up around the stuffing to enclose the stuffing, and tie the rolled pork in several places with kitchen twine or secure with toothpicks.
7. Try to replace any stuffing that falls out of the roast as you roll it, by stuffing it into the ends of the rolled pork. Season the external part of the pork with salt and freshly ground black pepper.
8. Preheat the air fryer to 182 degree C.
9. Place the stuffed pork loin into the air fryer, seam side down. Air-fry the pork loin for 15 minutes at 182 degree C. Turn the pork loin over and air-fry for an additional 15 minutes.
10. Turn the pork loin a quarter turn and air-fry for an additional 15 minutes. Turn the pork loin over again to expose the fourth side, and air-fry for an additional 10 minutes.
11. The pork loin should register 155°F on an instant read thermometer when it is finished.
12. While the pork is cooking, prepare the apple gravy. Preheat a saucepan over medium heat on the stovetop and melt the butter.
13. Add the shallot, apple and thyme sprigs and sauté until the apple starts to soften and brown a little.
14. Add the flour and stir for a minute or two. Whisk in the stock and apple cider vigorously to prevent the flour from forming lumps.

15. Boil mixture to thicken and season to taste with salt and pepper.
16. Transfer the pork loin to a resting plate and loosely tent with foil, letting the pork rest for at least 5 minutes before slicing and serving with the apple gravy poured over the top.

Nutrition: Calories: 546kcal; Carbs: 34g; Fat: 6g; Protein: 2g

47. Pork & Beef Egg Rolls

Preparation Time: 5 minutes

Cooking time: 8 minutes

Servings: 8

Ingredients:

- 113g very lean ground beef
- 113g lean ground pork
- 15g soy sauce
- 5ml olive oil
- 100g grated carrots
- 2 green onions, chopped
- 400g grated Napa cabbage
- 85g chopped water chestnuts
- 1.42g salt
- 1.42g garlic powder
- 1.42g black pepper
- 1 egg
- 15ml water
- 8 egg roll wraps
- oil for misting or cooking spray

Directions:

1. In a large skillet, brown beef and pork with soy sauce. Remove cooked meat from skillet, drain, and set aside.
2. Pour off any excess grease from skillet. Add olive oil, carrots, and onions. Sauté until barely tender, about 1 minute.
3. Stir in cabbage, cover, and cook for 1 minute or just until cabbage slightly wilts. Remove from heat.
4. In a large bowl, combine the cooked meats and vegetables, water chestnuts, salt, garlic powder, and pepper. Stir well. If needed, add more salt to taste.
5. Beat together egg and water in a small bowl.
6. Fill egg roll wrappers, using about 85g of filling for each wrap. Roll up and brush all over with egg wash to seal. Spray very lightly with olive oil or cooking spray.

7. Place 4 egg rolls in air fryer basket and cook at 198 degree C for 4minutes. Turnover and cook 4 more minutes, until golden brown and crispy.

8. Repeat to cook remaining egg rolls.

Nutrition: Calories: 320kcal; Carbs: 14g; Fat: 10g; Protein: 2g

48. Italian Sausage Bake

Preparation Time: 10 minutes

Cooking time: 25 minutes

Servings: 4

Ingredients:

- 240g red bell pepper, strips
- 340g Italian sausage, sliced
- 100g minced onions
- 42g brown sugar
- 113g ketchup
- 28.3g mustard
- 28.3g apple cider vinegar
- 100g chicken broth

Directions:

1. Preheat air fryer to 176 degree C. Combine the Italian sausage, bell pepper, and minced onion into a bowl. Stir well.

2. Mix together brown sugar, ketchup, mustard, apple cider vinegar, and chicken broth in a small bowl. Pour over the sausage.

3. Place the bowl in the air fryer, and Bake until the sausage is hot, the vegetables are tender, and the sauce is bubbling and thickened, 10-15 minutes. Serve and enjoy!

Nutrition: Calories: 276kcal; Carbs: 16g; Fat: 10g; Protein: 2g

49. Tarragon Pork Tenderloin

Preparation Time: 5 minutes

Cooking time: 25 minutes

Servings: 4

Ingredients:

- 2.84g dried tarragon
- 453g pork tenderloin, sliced
- Salt and pepper to taste

- 28.3g Dijon mustard
- 1 clove garlic, minced
- 240g bread crumbs
- 28.3ml olive oil

Directions:

1. Preheat air fryer to 198 degree C. Using a rolling pin, pound the pork slices until they are about ¾ inch thick.
2. Season both sides with salt and pepper. Coat the pork with mustard and season with garlic and tarragon.
3. In a shallow basin, mix bread crumbs and olive oil. Dredge the pork with the bread crumbs, pressing firmly, so that it adheres.
4. Put the pork in the frying basket and Air Fry until the pork outside is brown and crisp, 12-14 minutes. Serve warm.

Nutrition: Calories: 546kcal; Carbs: 34g; Fat: 6g; Protein: 2g

50. Honey Mustard Pork Roast

Preparation Time: 10 minutes

Cooking time: 40 minutes

Servings: 4

Ingredients:

- 1 boneless pork loin roast
- 28.3g Dijon mustard
- 8.4g olive oil
- 5g honey
- 1 garlic clove, minced
- Salt and pepper to taste
- 5g dried rosemary

Directions:

1. Preheat air fryer to 176 degree C. Whisk all ingredients in a bowl. Massage into loin on all sides.
2. Place the loin in the frying basket and Roast for 40 minutes, turning once. Let sit onto a cutting board for 5 minutes before slicing. Serve.

Nutrition: Calories: 209kcal; Carbs: 14g; Fat: 6g; Protein: 2g

51. Meat Loaves

Preparation Time: 5 minutes

Cooking time: 19 minutes

Servings: 4

Ingredients:

Sauce:

- 85g white vinegar
- 85g brown sugar
- 28.3g Worcestershire sauce
- 100g ketchup

Meat Loaves

- 453g very lean ground beef
- 227g dry bread (approx. 1 slice torn into small pieces)
- 1 egg
- 113g minced onion
- 5g salt
- 28.3g ketchup

Directions:

1. In a small saucepan, combine all sauce ingredients and bring to a boil. Remove from heat and stir to ensure that brown sugar dissolves completely.
2. In a large bowl, combine the beef, bread, egg, onion, salt, and ketchup. Mix well.
3. Divide meat mixture into 4 portions and shape each into a thick, round patty. Patties will be about 3 to 3½ inches in diameter, and all four should fit easily into the air fryer basket at once.
4. Cook at 182 degree C for 18 minutes, until meat is well done. Baste tops of mini loaves with a small amount of sauce, and cook 1 minute.
5. Serve hot with additional sauce on the side.

Nutrition: Calories: 321kcal; Carbs: 29g; Fat: 16g; Protein: 2g

52.   Crispy Smoked Pork Chops

Preparation Time: 5 minutes

Cooking time: 8 minutes

Servings: 3

Ingredients:

- 227g All-purpose flour or tapioca flour
- 1 Large egg white(s)
- 28.3ml Water
- 1100gs Corn flake crumbs (gluten-free, if a concern)
- 3 ½-pound, ½-inch-thick bone-in smoked pork chops

Directions:

1. Preheat the air fryer to 190 degree C.
2. Set up and fill three shallow soup plates or small pie plates on your counter: one for the flour; one for the egg white(s), whisked with the water until foamy; and one for the corn flake crumbs.
3. Set a chop in the flour and turn it several times, coating both sides and the edges. Gently shake off any excess flour, then set it in the beaten egg white mixture.
4. Turn to coat both sides as well as the edges. Let any excess egg white slip back into the rest, then set the chop in the corn flake crumbs.
5. Turn it several times, pressing gently to coat the chop evenly on both sides and around the edge. Set the chop aside and continue coating the remaining chop(s) in the same way.
6. Set the chops in the basket with as much air space between them as possible. Air-fry undisturbed for 8 minutes, or until the coating is crunchy and the chops are heated through.
7. Use kitchen tongs to transfer the chops to a wire rack and cool for a couple of minutes before serving.

Nutrition: Calories: 311kcal; Carbs: 21g; Fat: 12g; Protein: 4g

53. Rosemary Lamb Chops

Preparation Time: 5 minutes

Cooking time: 6 minutes

Servings: 4

Ingredients:

- 8 lamb chops
- 15ml extra-virgin olive oil
- 5g dried rosemary, crushed
- 2 cloves garlic, minced
- 5g sea salt
- 1.42g black pepper

Directions:

1. In a large bowl, mix together the lamb chops, olive oil, rosemary, garlic, salt, and pepper. Leave in room temperature for 10 minutes.
2. Meanwhile, heat the air fryer to 193 degree C.
3. Cook the lamb chops for 3 minutes, flip them over, and cook for another 3 minutes.

Nutrition: Calories: 398kcal; Carbs: 23g; Fat: 8g; Protein: 6g

54. Mushroom & Quinoa-stuffed Pork Loins

Preparation Time: 10 minutes

Cooking time: 25 minutes

Servings: 3

Ingredients:

- 3 boneless center-cut pork loins, pocket cut in each loin
- 100g diced white mushrooms
- 5ml vegetable oil
- 3 bacon slices, diced
- ½ onion, peeled and diced
- 240g baby spinach
- Salt and pepper to taste
- 100g cooked quinoa
- 100g mozzarella cheese

Directions:

1. Warm the oil in a skillet over medium heat. Add the bacon and cook for 3 minutes until the fat is rendered but not crispy.
2. Add in onion and mushrooms and stir-fry for 3 minutes until the onions are translucent. Stir in spinach, salt, and pepper and cook for 1 minute until the spinach wilts. Set aside and toss in quinoa.
3. Preheat air fryer at 176 degree C. Stuff quinoa mixture into each pork loin and sprinkle with mozzarella cheese. Place them in the frying basket and Air Fry for 11 minutes. Let rest onto a cutting board for 5 minutes before serving.

Nutrition: Calories: 287kcal; Carbs: 24g; Fat: 9g; Protein: 2g

55. Indian Fry Bread Tacos

Preparation Time: 10 minutes

Cooking time: 20 minutes

Servings: 4

Ingredients:

- 240g all-purpose flour
- 12.84gs salt, divided
- 12.84gs baking powder
- 85ml milk
- 85ml warm water
- 226g lean ground beef
- One 14.5-ounce can pinto beans, drained and rinsed
- 15g taco seasoning
- 100g shredded cheddar cheese
- 400g shredded lettuce
- 85g black olives, chopped

- 1 Roma tomato, diced
- 1 avocado, diced
- 1 lime

Directions:

1. In a large basin, whisk together the flour, 5g of the salt, and baking powder. Make a hole in the center and add in the milk and water. Form a ball and gently knead the dough four times. Cover the bowl with a damp towel, and set aside.

2. Preheat the air fryer to 193 degree C.

3. In a medium bowl, mix together the ground beef, beans, and taco seasoning. Crumble the meat mixture into the air fryer basket and cook for 5 minutes; toss the meat and cook an additional 2 to 3 minutes, or until cooked fully. Place the cooked meat in a bowl for taco assembly; season with the remaining 2.84g salt as desired.

4. On a floured surface, place the dough. Cut the dough into 4 equal parts. Using a rolling pin, roll out each piece of dough to 5 inches in diameter.

5. Spray the dough with cooking spray and place in the air fryer basket, working in batches as needed. Cook for 3 minutes, flip over, spray with cooking spray, and cook for an additional 1 to 3 minutes, until golden and puffy.

6. To assemble, place the fry breads on a serving platter. Equally divide the meat and bean mixture on top of the fry bread.

7. Divide the cheese, lettuce, olives, tomatoes, and avocado among the four tacos. Squeeze lime over the top prior to serving.

Nutrition: Calories: 546kcal; Carbs: 34g; Fat: 6g; Protein: 2g

56. Beef Short Ribs

Preparation Time: 5 minutes

Cooking time: 20 minutes

Servings: 4

Ingredients:

- 28.3g soy sauce
- 15ml sesame oil
- 28.3g brown sugar
- 5g ground ginger
- 2 garlic cloves, crushed
- 453g beef short ribs

Directions:

1. In a small basin, mix together the soy sauce, sesame oil, brown sugar, and ginger. Transfer the mixture to a large resealable plastic bag, and place the garlic cloves and short ribs into the bag. Secure and place in the refrigerator for an hour (or overnight).

2. When you're ready to prepare the dish, preheat the air fryer to 165 degree C.

3. Liberally spray the air fryer basket with olive oil mist and set the beef short ribs in the basket.

4. Cook for 10 minutes, flip the short ribs, and then cook another 10 minutes.

5. Remove the short ribs from the air fryer basket, loosely cover with aluminum foil, and let them rest. The short ribs will continue to cook after they're removed from the basket.

6. Check the internal temperature after 5 minutes to make sure it reached 145°F if you prefer a well-done meat.

7. If it didn't reach 145°F and you would like it to be cooked longer, you can put it back into the air fryer basket at 165 degree C for another 3 minutes.

8. Remove from the basket and let it rest, covered with aluminum foil, for 5 minutes. Serve immediately.

Nutrition: Calories: 321kcal; Carbs: 21g; Fat: 7g; Protein: 8g

57. Wasabi Pork Medallions

Preparation Time: 5 minutes

Cooking time: 16 minutes

Servings: 4

Ingredients:

- 453g pork medallions
- 240g soy sauce
- 15g mirin
- 100ml olive oil
- 3 cloves garlic, crushed
- 5g fresh grated ginger
- 5g wasabi paste
- 15g brown sugar

Directions:

1. Place all ingredients, except for the pork, in a resealable bag and shake to combine. Add the pork medallions to the bag, shake again, and place in the fridge to marinate for 2 hours.
2. Preheat air fryer to 182 degree C. Remove pork medallions from the marinade and place them in the frying basket in rows.
3. Air Fry for 14-16 minutes or until the medallions are cooked through and juicy. Serve.

Nutrition: Calories: 234kcal; Carbs: 24g; Fat: 9g; Protein: 4g

58. Spicy Hoisin Bbq Pork Chops

Preparation Time: 5 minutes

Cooking time: 12 minutes

Servings: 2

Ingredients:

- 42.52g hoisin sauce
- 85g honey
- 15g soy sauce
- 42.52g rice vinegar
- 28.3g brown sugar
- 12.84gs grated fresh ginger
- 1 to 8.4g Sriracha sauce, to taste
- 2 to 3 bone-in center cut pork chops, 1-inch thick (about 1113gs)
- chopped scallions, for garnish

Directions:

1. Combine the hoisin sauce, honey, soy sauce, rice vinegar, brown sugar, ginger, and Sriracha sauce in a small saucepan.
2. Whisk the ingredients together and bring the mixture to a boil over medium-high heat on the stovetop.
3. Lower the heat and simmer the sauce until it has reduced in volume and thickened slightly – about 10 minutes.
4. Preheat the air fryer to 204 degree C.
5. Put the pork chops into the air fryer basket and pour half the hoisin BBQ sauce over the top. Air-fry for 6 minutes.
6. Then, flip the chops over, pour the remaining hoisin BBQ sauce on top and air-fry for 6 more minutes, depending on the thickness of the pork chops. The internal temp of the pork chops should be 155°F when tested with an instant read thermometer.
7. Let the pork chops rest for 5 minutes before serving. You can spoon a little of the sauce from the bottom drawer of the air fryer over the top if desired. Sprinkle with chopped scallions and serve.

Nutrition: Calories: 278kcal; Carbs: 18g; Fat: 10g; Protein: 3g

59. French-style Pork Medallions

Preparation Time: 5 minutes

Cooking time: 25 minutes

Servings: 4

Ingredients:

- 453g pork medallions
- Salt and pepper to taste
- 2.84g dried marjoram

- 28.3g butter
- 15ml olive oil
- 5g garlic powder
- 1 shallot, diced
- 200g chicken stock
- 28.3g Dijon mustard
- 28.3g grainy mustard
- 1/3 cup heavy cream

Directions:

1. Preheat the air fryer to 176 degree C. Pound the pork medallions with a rolling pin to about ¼ inch thickness. Rub them with salt, pepper, garlic, and marjoram.

2. Place into the greased frying basket and Bake for 7 minutes or until almost done. Remove and wipe the basket clean.

3. Combine the butter, olive oil, shallot, and stock in a baking pan, and set it in the frying basket.

4. Bake for 5 minutes or until the shallot is crispy and tender. Add the mustard and heavy cream and cook for 4 more minutes or until the mix starts to thicken.

5. Then add the pork to the sauce and cook for 5 more minutes, or until the sauce simmers. Remove and serve warm.

Nutrition: Calories: 234kcal; Carbs: 14g; Fat: 6g; Protein: 5g

60. Basil Cheese & Ham Stromboli

Preparation Time: 10 minutes

Cooking time: 30 minutes

Servings: 6

Ingredients:

- 1 can refrigerated pizza dough
- 100g shredded mozzarella
- ½ red bell pepper, sliced
- 8.4g all-purpose flour
- 6 Havarti cheese slices
- 12 deli ham slices
- 2.84g dried basil
- 5g garlic powder
- 2.84g oregano
- Black pepper to taste

Directions:

1. Preheat air fryer to 204 degree C. Flour a flat work surface and roll out the pizza dough. Use a knife to cut into 6 equal-sized rectangles.
2. On each rectangle, add 1 slice of Havarti, 15g of mozzarella, 2 slices of ham, and some red pepper slices.
3. Season with basil, garlic, oregano, and black pepper. Fold one side of the dough over the filling to the opposite side.
4. Press the edges with the back of a fork to seal them. Place one batch of stromboli in the fryer and lightly spray with cooking oil. Air Fry for 10 minutes. Serve and enjoy!

Nutrition: Calories: 320kcal; Carbs: 24g; Fat: 6g; Protein: 8g

CHAPTER 4: Seafood

61. Lemony Shrimp and Zucchini

Preparation Time: 15 minutes

Cooking time: 7-8 minutes

Servings: 4

Ingredients:

- 600 g extra-large raw shrimp, peeled and deveined
- 2 medium zucchini (about 250 g / 227 g each), halved lengthwise and cut into ½-inch-thick slices
- 20g olive oil
- 2.84g garlic salt
- 12.84gs dried oregano
- 1/8 teaspoon crushed red pepper flakes (optional)
- Juice of ½ lemon
- 15g chopped fresh mint
- 15g chopped fresh dill

Directions:

1. Combine the shrimp, zucchini, oil, garlic salt, oregano, and pepper flakes (if using) in a large bowl, and toss to coat.
2. Arrange a single layer of the shrimp and zucchini in the air fryer basket, if working in batches. Air fry at 176 degree C for 7 to 8 minutes, shaking the basket halfway until the zucchini is golden and the shrimp are cooked through.
3. Move it to a serving dish then tent with foil while you air fry the remaining shrimp and zucchini. Top with lemon juice, mint, and dill and serve.

Nutrition: Calories: 443kcal, Carbs: 79g, Fat: 8g, Protein: 13g

62. Lime-Chili Shrimp Bowl

Preparation Time: 10 minutes

Cooking time: 10-15 minutes

Servings: 4

Ingredients:

- 8.4g lime juice
- 5ml olive oil
- 5g honey
- 5g minced garlic
- 5g chili powder
- Salt, to taste
- 350 g medium shrimp, peeled and deveined
- 500 g cooked brown rice
- 450 g can seasoned black beans, warmed
- 1 large avocado, chopped
- 250 g sliced cherry tomatoes
- Cooking spray

Directions:

1. Spray the air fryer basket lightly with cooking spray. Mix the lime juice, olive oil, honey, garlic, chili powder, and salt in a medium bowl, to make a marinade.
2. Put the shrimp then toss to coat evenly in the marinade.
3. Place the shrimp in the air fryer basket. Air fry at 204ºC for 5 minutes. Shake the basket and air fry until the shrimp are cooked through and starting to brown, an additional 5 to 10 minutes.
4. To assemble the bowls, spoon ¼ of the rice, black beans, avocado, and cherry tomatoes into each of the four bowls. Top with the shrimp and serve.

Nutrition: Calories: 395kcal, Carbs: 52g, Fat: 5g, Protein: 41g

63.   Marinated Salmon Fillets

Preparation Time: 10 minutes

Cooking time: 15-20 minutes

Servings: 4

Ingredients:

- 50 g soy sauce
- 50 g rice wine vinegar
- 15g brown sugar
- 15ml olive oil
- 5g mustard powder
- 5g ground ginger
- 2.84g freshly ground black pepper
- 2.84g minced garlic
- 4 (175 g) salmon fillets, skin-on
- Cooking spray

Directions:

1. Combine the rice wine vinegar, brown sugar, soy sauce, olive oil, mustard powder, ginger, black pepper, and garlic in a small bowl, to make a marinade.

2. Place the fillets in a shallow baking dish and pour the marinade over them. Cover the baking dish and marinate for at least 1 hour in the refrigerator, turning the fillets occasionally to keep them coated in the marinade.

3. Spray the air fryer basket lightly with cooking spray. Shake off the marinade as possible from the fillets and place them, skin-side down, in the air fryer basket in a single layer.

4. You may need to cook the fillets in batches. Air fry at 188ºC for 15 to 20 minutes for well done. Serve hot.

Nutrition: Calories: 360kcal, Carbs: 2g, Fat: 22g, Protein: 40g

64. New Orleans-Style Crab Cakes

Preparation Time: 10 minutes

Cooking time: 8-10 minutes

Servings: 4

Ingredients:

- 300 g bread crumbs
- 8.4g Creole Seasoning
- 5g dry mustard
- 5g salt
- 5g freshly ground black pepper
- 350 g crab meat
- 2 large eggs, beaten
- 5g butter, melted
- 80 g minced onion
- Cooking spray
- Pecan Tartar Sauce, for serving

Directions:

1. Prepare your air fryer basket with parchment paper. In a medium bowl, whisk the bread crumbs, Creole Seasoning, dry mustard, salt, and pepper until blended.

2. Add the crab meat, eggs, butter, and onion. Stir until blended. Shape the crab mixture into 8 patties. Place the crab cakes on the parchment and spritz with oil.

3. Air fry at 176 degree C for 4 minutes. Flip the cakes, spritz them with oil, and air fry for 4 to 6 minutes more until the outsides are firm and a fork inserted into the center comes out clean.

4. Serve with the Pecan Tartar Sauce.

Nutrition: Calories: 150kcal, Carbs: 17g, Fat: 3g, Protein: 15g

65. Oyster Po'Boy

Preparation Time: 20 minutes

Cooking time: 5 minutes

Servings: 4

Ingredients:

- 175 g all-purpose flour
- 50 g yellow cornmeal
- 15g Cajun seasoning
- 5g salt
- 2 large eggs, beaten
- 5g hot sauce
- 450 g pre-shucked oysters
- 1 (12-inch) French baguette, quartered and sliced horizontally
- Tartar Sauce, as needed
- 500 g shredded lettuce, divided
- 2 tomatoes, cut into slices
- Cooking spray

Directions:

1. In a shallow bowl, whisk the flour, cornmeal, Cajun seasoning, and salt until blended. In a second shallow bowl, whisk together the eggs and hot sauce.
2. One at a time, dip the oysters in the cornmeal mixture, the eggs, and again in the cornmeal, coating thoroughly.
3. Prepare your air fryer basket with parchment paper. Place the oysters on the parchment and spritz with oil.
4. Air fry at 204ºC for 2 minutes. Shake the basket, spritz the oysters with oil, and air fry for 3 minutes more until lightly browned and crispy.
5. Spread each sandwich half with Tartar Sauce. Assemble the po'boys by layering each sandwich with fried oysters, 100 g shredded lettuce, and 2 tomato slices. Serve immediately.

Nutrition: Calories: 740kcal, Carbs: 78g, Fat: 41g, Protein: 18g

66. Pecan-Crusted Tilapia

Preparation Time: 10 minutes

Cooking time: 10 minutes

Servings: 4

Ingredients:

- 300 g pecans
- 175 g panko bread crumbs
- 100 g all-purpose flour

- 28.3g Cajun seasoning
- 2 eggs, beaten with 28.3g water
- 4 (175 g) tilapia fillets
- Vegetable oil, for spraying
- Lemon wedges, for serving

Directions:

1. Grind the pecans in the food processor until they resemble coarse meals. Combine the ground pecans with the panko on a plate.

2. On a second plate, combine the flour and Cajun seasoning. Dry the tilapia fillets using paper towels and dredge them in the flour mixture, shaking off any excess.

3. Dip the fillets in the egg mixture and then dredge them in the pecan and panko mixture, pressing the coating onto the fillets. Put the breaded fillets on a plate or rack.

4. Spray both sides of the breaded fillets with oil. Carefully transfer 2 of the fillets to the air fryer basket and air fry at 191ºC for 9 to 10 minutes, flipping once halfway through, until the flesh is opaque and flaky. Repeat with the remaining fillets.

5. Serve immediately with lemon wedges.

Nutrition: Calories: 360kcal, Carbs: 18g, Fat: 21g, Protein: 29g

67. Remoulade Crab Cakes

Preparation Time: 15 minutes

Cooking time: 10 minutes

Servings: 4

Ingredients:

Remoulade:

- 175 g mayonnaise
- 8.4g Dijon mustard
- 12.84gs yellow mustard
- 5g vinegar
- 1.42g hot sauce
- 5g tiny capers, drained and chopped
- 1.42g salt
- 1/8 teaspoon ground black pepper

Crab Cakes:

- 250 g bread crumbs, divided
- 28.3g mayonnaise
- 1 scallion, finely chopped

- 175 g crab meat
- 28.3g pasteurized egg product (liquid eggs in a carton)
- 8.4ml lemon juice
- 2.84g red pepper flakes
- 2.84g Old Bay seasoning
- Cooking spray

Directions:

1. Whisk to combine the mayonnaise, Dijon mustard, yellow mustard, vinegar, hot sauce, capers, salt, and pepper in a small bowl.
2. Refrigerate for at least 1 hour before serving. Place a parchment liner in the air fryer basket.
3. In a large bowl, mix to combine 100g of bread crumbs with the mayonnaise and scallion. Set the other 100g of bread crumbs aside in a small bowl.
4. Add the crab meat, egg product, lemon juice, red pepper flakes, and Old Bay seasoning to the large bowl, and stir to combine.
5. Divide the crab batter into 4 portions, and form it into patties. Dredge each patty in the remaining bread crumbs to coat. Place the prepared patties on the liner in the air fryer in a single layer.
6. Spray lightly with cooking spray and air fry at 204ºC for 5 minutes. Flip the crab cakes over, air fry for another 5 minutes, until golden, and serve.

Nutrition: Calories: 200kcal, Carbs: 5g, Fat: 22g, Protein: 19g

68. Roasted Fish with Almond-Lemon Crumbs

Preparation Time: 15 minutes

Cooking time: 7-8 minutes

Servings: 4

Ingredients:

- 100 g raw whole almonds
- 1 scallion, finely chopped
- Grated zest and juice of 1 lemon
- ½ tablespoon extra-virgin olive oil
- 3.7g kosher salt, divided
- Freshly ground black pepper, to taste
- 4 (175 g each) skinless fish fillets
- Cooking spray
- 5g Dijon mustard

Directions:

1. Pulse the almonds to coarsely chop in a food processor. Move it to a small bowl then put the scallion, lemon zest, and olive oil. Season with 1.42g of salt and pepper to taste and mix to combine.

2. Spray the top of the fish with oil and squeeze the lemon juice over the fish. Season with the remaining 2.84g salt and pepper to taste.

3. Spread the mustard on top of your fish. Dividing evenly, press the almond mixture onto the top of the fillets to adhere.

4. Working in batches, place the fillets in the air fryer basket in a single layer. Air fry at 191ºC for 7 to 8 minutes, until the crumbs start to brown and the fish is cooked through. Serve immediately.

Nutrition: Calories: 282kcal, Carbs: 6g, Fat: 13g, Protein: 36g

69. Salmon Burgers

Preparation Time: 15 minutes

Cooking time: 12 minutes

Servings: 5

Ingredients:

Lemon-Caper Rémoulade:

- 100 g mayonnaise
- 28.3g minced drained capers
- 28.3g chopped fresh parsley
- 8.4ml fresh lemon juice

Salmon Patties:

- 450 g wild salmon fillet, skinned and pin bones removed
- 85g panko bread crumbs
- 50 g minced red onion plus 50 g slivered for serving
- 1 garlic clove, minced
- 1 large egg, lightly beaten
- 15g Dijon mustard
- 5g fresh lemon juice
- 15g chopped fresh parsley
- 2.84g kosher salt

For Serving:

- 5 whole wheat potato buns or gluten-free buns
- 10 butter lettuce leaves

Directions:

1. For the lemon-caper rémoulade: In a small bowl, combine the mayonnaise, capers, parsley, and lemon juice and mix well.

2. For the salmon patties: Cut off a 100 g piece of the salmon and transfer to a food processor. Pulse until it becomes pasty. With a sharp knife, chop the remaining salmon into small cubes.

3. In a medium bowl, combine the chopped and processed salmon with the panko, minced red onion, garlic, egg, mustard, lemon juice, parsley, and salt.

4. Toss gently to combine. Form the mixture into 5 patties about ¾ inch thick. Refrigerate for at least 30 minutes.

5. Put the patties in the air fryer basket. Air fry at 204ºC for about 12 minutes, gently flipping halfway, until golden and cooked through.

6. To serve, transfer each patty to a bun. Top each with 2 lettuce leaves, 28.3g of the rémoulade, and the slivered red onions.

Nutrition: Calories: 130kcal, Carbs: 0g, Fat: 6g, Protein: 21g

70. Salmon Patties

Preparation Time: 10 minutes

Cooking time: 8 minutes

Servings: 4

Ingredients:

- 2 (150 g) cans salmon, flaked
- 2 large eggs, beaten
- 80 g minced onion
- 150 g panko bread crumbs
- 12.84gs Italian-Style seasoning
- 5g garlic powder
- Cooking spray

Directions:

1. In a medium bowl, stir together the salmon, eggs, and onion. In a small bowl, whisk the bread crumbs, Italian-Style seasoning, and garlic powder until blended.

2. Add the bread crumb mixture to the salmon mixture and stir until blended. Shape the mixture into 8 patties. Line the air fryer basket with parchment paper.

3. Working in batches as needed, place the patties on the parchment and spritz with oil. Bake at 176 degree C for 4 minutes.

4. Flip, spritz the patties with oil, and bake for 4 to 8 minutes more, until browned and firm. Serve.

Nutrition: Calories: 196kcal, Carbs: 15g, Fat: 9g, Protein: 16g

71.Seasoned Breaded Shrimp

Preparation Time: 15 minutes

Cooking time: 10-15 minutes

Servings: 4

Ingredients:

- 8.4g Old Bay seasoning, divided
- 2.84g garlic powder
- 2.84g onion powder
- 450 g large shrimp, deveined, with tails on
- 2 large eggs
- 100 g whole-wheat panko bread crumbs
- Cooking spray

Directions:

1. Spray the air fryer basket lightly with cooking spray. In a medium bowl, mix together 5g of Old Bay seasoning, garlic powder, and onion powder.
2. Add the shrimp and toss with the seasoning mix to lightly coat. In a separate small bowl, whisk the eggs with 5g water.
3. In a shallow bowl, mix together the remaining 5g Old Bay seasoning and the panko bread crumbs.
4. Dip each shrimp in the egg batter and dredge in the bread crumb mixture to evenly coat.
5. Place the shrimp in the air fryer basket, in a single layer. Lightly spray the shrimp with cooking spray. You may need to cook the shrimp in batches.
6. Air fry at 193ºC for 10 to 15 minutes, or until the shrimp is cooked through and crispy, shaking the basket at 5-minute intervals to redistribute and evenly cook. Serve immediately.

Nutrition: Calories: 150kcal, Carbs: 25g, Fat: 2g, Protein: 10g

72. Spanish Garlic Shrimp

Preparation Time: 15 minutes

Cooking time: 10-15 minutes

Servings: 4

Ingredients:

- 8.4g minced garlic
- 8.4ml lemon juice
- 8.4ml olive oil
- ½ to 5g crushed red pepper
- 350 g medium shrimp, deveined, with tails on
- Cooking spray

Directions:

1. In a medium bowl, mix together the garlic, lemon juice, olive oil, and crushed red pepper to make a marinade.
2. Put the shrimp then toss to coat in the marinade. Cover with plastic wrap and place the bowl in the refrigerator for 30 minutes. Spray the air fryer basket lightly with cooking spray.

3. Place the shrimp in the air fryer basket. Air fry at 204ºC for 5 minutes. Shake the basket and air fry until the shrimp are cooked through and nicely browned, an additional 5 to 10 minutes. Cool for 5 minutes before serving.

Nutrition: Calories: 130kcal, Carbs: 3g, Fat: 4g, Protein: 17g

73. Spicy Orange Shrimp

Preparation Time: 20 minutes

Cooking time: 10-15 minutes

Servings: 4

Ingredients:

- 80ml orange juice
- 3 teaspoons minced garlic
- 5g Old Bay seasoning
- ¼ to 2.84g cayenne pepper
- 450 g medium shrimp, peeled and deveined, with tails off
- Cooking spray

Directions:

1. In a medium bowl, combine the orange juice, garlic, old Bay seasoning, and cayenne pepper. Dry the shrimp using a paper towel to remove excess water.

2. Put the shrimp to your marinade then stir to evenly coat. Wrap it using plastic wrap and place it in the refrigerator for 30 minutes so the shrimp can soak up the marinade.

3. Spray the air fryer basket lightly with cooking spray. Put the shrimp into the air fryer basket. Air fry at 204ºC for 5 minutes. Shake the basket and lightly spray with olive oil.

4. Air fry until the shrimp are opaque and crisp, 5 to 10 more minutes. Serve immediately.

Nutrition: Calories: 139kcal, Carbs: 1g, Fat: 4g, Protein: 23g

74. Swordfish Skewers with Caponata

Preparation Time: 15 minutes

Cooking time: 20 minutes

Servings: 2

Ingredients:

- 300 g small Italian eggplant, cut into 1-inch pieces
- 175 g cherry tomatoes
- 3 scallions, cut into 2 inches long
- 28.3g extra-virgin olive oil, divided
- Salt and pepper, to taste
- 350 g skinless swordfish steaks, 1¼ inches thick, cut into 1-inch pieces
- 8.4g honey, divided
- 8.4g ground coriander, divided
- 5g grated lemon zest, divided
- 5ml juice
- 4 (6-inch) wooden skewers
- 1 garlic clove, minced
- 2.84g ground cumin
- 15g chopped fresh basil

Directions:

1. Toss eggplant, tomatoes, and scallions with 15g oil, 1.42g salt, and 1/8 teaspoon pepper in a bowl; transfer to air fryer basket.

2. Air fry at 204ºC until eggplant is softened and browned and tomatoes have begun to burst, about 14 minutes, tossing halfway through cooking. Transfer vegetables to cutting board and set aside to cool slightly.

3. Pat swordfish dry with paper towels. Combine 5g oil, 5g honey, 5g coriander, 2.84g lemon zest, 1/8 teaspoon salt, and pinch pepper in a clean bowl.

4. Add swordfish and toss to coat. Thread swordfish onto skewers, leaving about ¼ inch between each piece (3 or 4 pieces per skewer).

5. Arrange skewers in the air fryer basket, spaced evenly apart. (Skewers may overlap slightly.)

6. Return basket to air fryer and air fry at 400ºF (204ºC) until swordfish is browned and registers 60ºC, 6 to 8 minutes, flipping and rotating skewers halfway through cooking.

7. Meanwhile, combine remaining 8.4g oil, remaining 5g honey, remaining 5g coriander, remaining 2.84g lemon zest, lemon juice, garlic, cumin, 1.42g salt, and 1/8 teaspoon pepper in a large bowl.

8. Microwave, stirring once, until fragrant, about 30 seconds. Coarsely chop the cooked vegetables, transfer to bowl with dressing, along with any accumulated juices, and gently toss to combine.

9. Stir in basil and season with salt and pepper to taste. Serve skewers with caponata.

Nutrition: Calories: 109kcal, Carbs: 8g, Fat: 5g, Protein: 8g

75. Tandoori-Spiced Salmon and Potatoes

Preparation Time: 10 minutes

Cooking time: 28 minutes

Servings: 2

Ingredients:

- 450 g fingerling potatoes
- 28.3ml vegetable oil, divided
- Kosher salt, to taste
- freshly ground black pepper, to taste
- 5g ground turmeric
- 5g ground cumin
- 5g ground ginger
- 2.84g smoked paprika
- 1.42g cayenne pepper
- 2 (175 g) skin-on salmon fillets

Directions:

1. Toss the potatoes with one tablespoon of the oil until evenly coated in a bowl. Season with salt and pepper. Move the potatoes to your air fryer and air fry at 191ºC for 20 minutes.
2. Meanwhile, in a bowl, combine the remaining 15ml oil, the turmeric, cumin, ginger, paprika, and cayenne. Add the salmon fillets and turn in the spice mixture until fully coated all over.
3. After the potatoes have air fried for 20 minutes, place the salmon fillets, skin-side up, on top of the potatoes, and continue cooking until the potatoes are tender, the salmon is cooked, and the salmon skin is slightly crisp.
4. Transfer the salmon fillets to two plates and serve with the potatoes while both are warm.

Nutrition: Calories: 504kcal, Carbs: 29g, Fat: 25g, Protein: 30g

76. Tortilla Shrimp Tacos

Preparation Time: 10 minutes

Cooking time: 6 minutes

Servings: 4

Ingredients:

Spicy Mayo:

- 42.52g mayonnaise
- 15g Louisiana-style hot pepper sauce

- Cilantro-Lime Slaw:
- 500 g shredded green cabbage
- ½ small red onion, thinly sliced
- 1 small jalapeño, thinly sliced
- 28.3g chopped fresh cilantro
- Juice of 1 lime
- 1.42g kosher salt

Shrimp:

- 1 large egg, beaten
- 250 g crushed tortilla chips
- 24 jumbo shrimp (450 g), peeled and deveined
- 1/8 teaspoon kosher salt
- Cooking spray
- 8 corn tortillas, for serving

Directions:

1. For the spicy mayo, mix the mayonnaise and hot pepper sauce in a small bowl. For the cilantro-lime slaw: In a large bowl, toss together the cabbage, onion, jalapeño, cilantro, lime juice, and salt to combine. Cover and refrigerate to chill.
2. For the shrimp: Place the egg in a shallow bowl and the crushed tortilla chips in another. Season the shrimp with salt.
3. Dip the shrimp in the egg, then in the crumbs, pressing gently to adhere. Place on a work surface and spray both sides with oil.
4. Working in batches, arrange a single layer of the shrimp in the air fryer basket. Air fry at 182ºC for 6 minutes, flipping halfway, until golden and cooked through in the center.
5. Put two tortillas on each plate and top each with 3 shrimp. Top each taco with 50 g slaw, then drizzle with spicy mayo.

Nutrition: Calories: 250kcal, Carbs: 23g, Fat: 9g, Protein: 22g

77. Traditional Tuna Melt

Preparation Time: 10 minutes

Cooking time: 12 minutes

Servings: 2

Ingredients:

- 2 cans unsalted albacore tuna, drained
- 100 g mayonnaise
- 2.84g salt

- 1.42g ground black pepper
- 4 slices sourdough bread
- 4 pieces sliced Cheddar cheese
- 28.3g crispy fried onions
- Cooking spray
- 1.42g granulated garlic

Directions:

1. Combine the tuna, mayonnaise, salt, and pepper in a medium bowl, and mix well. Set aside. Assemble the sandwiches by laying out the bread and then adding 1 slice of cheese on top of each piece.
2. Sprinkle your fried onions on top of the cheese on 2 of the slices of bread. Divide the tuna between the 2 slices of bread with the onions.
3. Take the remaining 2 slices of bread that have only cheese on them, and place them cheese-side down on top of the tuna.
4. Place one sandwich in the air fryer basket, spray with cooking spray, and air fry at 199ºC for 6 minutes.
5. Using a spatula, flip the sandwich over, spray it again, and air fry for another 6 minutes, or until golden brown.
6. Sprinkle with the garlic immediately after removing it from the air fryer basket. Repeat with the other sandwich. Allow the sandwiches to sit for 1 to 2 minutes before cutting and serving.

Nutrition: Calories: 290kcal, Carbs: 28g, Fat: 8g, Protein: 30g

78. Trout Amandine with Lemon Butter Sauce

Preparation Time: 20 minutes

Cooking time: 8 minutes

Servings: 4

Ingredients:

Trout Amandine:

- 150 g toasted almonds
- 80 g grated Parmesan cheese
- 5g salt
- 2.84g freshly ground black pepper
- 28.3g butter, melted
- 4 (100 g) trout fillets, or salmon fillets
- Cooking spray

Lemon Butter Sauce:

- 8 tablespoons (1 stick) butter, melted
- 28.3g freshly squeezed lemon juice

- 2.84g Worcestershire sauce
- 2.84g salt
- 2.84g freshly ground black pepper
- 1.42g hot sauce

Directions:

1. Pulse the almonds for 5 to 10 seconds until finely processed in a blender or food processor.
2. Transfer to a shallow bowl and whisk in the Parmesan cheese, salt, and pepper. Place the melted butter in another shallow bowl.
3. One at a time, dip the fish in the melted butter, then the almond mixture, coating thoroughly.
4. Prepare your air fryer basket using parchment paper. Place the coated fish on the parchment and spritz with oil.
5. Bake at 149ºC for 4 minutes. Flip the fish, spritz it with oil, and bake for 4 minutes more until the fish flakes easily with a fork.
6. Whisk the butter, lemon juice, Worcestershire sauce, salt, pepper, and hot sauce until blended in a small bowl. Serve with the fish.

Nutrition: Calories: 238kcal, Carbs: 11g, Fat: 4g, Protein: 20g

79. Tuna Patty Sliders

Preparation Time: 15 minutes

Cooking time: 10-15 minutes

Servings: 4

Ingredients:

- 3 (150 g) cans tuna, packed in water
- 150 g whole-wheat panko bread crumbs
- 80 g shredded Parmesan cheese
- 15g sriracha
- 3.7g black pepper
- 10 whole-wheat slider buns
- Cooking spray

Directions:

1. Spray the air fryer basket lightly with cooking spray. Combine the tuna, bread crumbs, Parmesan cheese, sriracha, and black pepper in a medium bowl and stir to combine.
2. Form the mixture into 10 patties. Put the patties in your air fryer basket in a single layer. Spray the patties lightly with cooking spray. You may need to cook them in batches.
3. Air fry at 176 degree C for 6 to 8 minutes. Turn the patties over and lightly spray with cooking spray. Air fry until golden brown and crisp, another 4 to 7 more minutes. Serve warm.

Nutrition: Calories: 238kcal, Carbs: 11g, Fat: 4g, Protein: 20g

80. Tuna-Stuffed Quinoa Patties

Preparation Time: 10 minutes

Cooking time: 15 minutes

Servings: 4

Ingredients:

- 350 g quinoa
- 4 slices white bread with crusts removed
- 100 g milk
- 3 eggs
- 300 g tuna packed in olive oil, drained
- 2 to 3 lemons
- Kosher salt and pepper, to taste
- 300 g panko bread crumbs
- Vegetable oil, for spraying
- Lemon wedges, for serving

Directions:

1. Rinse your quinoa in a fine-mesh sieve until the water runs clear. Bring 1 liter of salted water to a boil. Add the quinoa, cover, and reduce heat to low.

2. Simmer the quinoa covered until most of the water is absorbed and the quinoa is tender for 15 to 20 minutes.

3. Drain then allow it to cool to room temperature. Meanwhile, soak the bread in the milk.

4. Mix the drained quinoa with the soaked bread and 2 of the eggs in a large bowl and mix thoroughly.

5. In a medium bowl, combine the tuna, the remaining egg, and the juice and zest of 1 of the lemons. Season well with salt and pepper. Spread the panko on a plate.

6. Scoop up approximately 100 g of the quinoa mixture and flatten it into a patty. Place a heaping tablespoon of the tuna mixture in the center of the patty and close the quinoa around the tuna.

7. Flatten the patty slightly to create an oval-shaped croquette. Dredge both sides of the croquette in the panko. Repeat with the remaining quinoa and tuna.

8. Oiled ay the air fryer basket using oil to prevent sticking. Arrange 4 or 5 of the croquettes in the basket, taking care to avoid overcrowding.

9. Spray the tops of the croquettes with oil. Air fry at 204ºC within 8 minutes until the top side is browned and crispy.

10. Carefully turn the croquettes over and spray the second side with oil. Air fry until the second side is browned and crispy, another 7 minutes. Repeat with the remaining croquettes.

11. Serve the croquetas warm with plenty of lemon wedges for spritzing.

Nutrition: Calories: 198kcal, Carbs: 26g, Fat: 4g, Protein: 15g

CHAPTER 5: **Vegetables**

81.Air Fried Green Beans

Preparation Time: 10 minutes

Cooking time: 10 minutes

Servings: 4

Ingredients:

- 700 g French green beans, stems removed and blanched
- 15g salt
- 225 g shallots, peeled and cut into quarters
- 2.84g ground white pepper
- 28.3ml olive oil

Directions:

1. Coat the vegetables with the rest of the ingredients in a bowl.
2. Transfer to the air fryer basket and Air Fry at 204ºC for 10 minutes, making sure the green beans achieve a light brown color. Serve hot.

Nutrition: Calories: 243kcal, Carbs: 30g, Fat: 12g, Protein: 5g

82. Black Bean Chili

Preparation Time: 15 minutes

Cooking time: 23 minutes

Servings: 6

Ingredients:

- 15ml olive oil
- 1 medium onion, diced
- 3 garlic cloves, minced
- 250 g vegetable broth
- 3 cans black beans, drained and rinsed
- 2 cans diced tomatoes
- 2 chipotle peppers, chopped
- 8.4g cumin
- 8.4g chili powder
- 5g dried oregano
- 2.84g salt

Directions:

1. Fry the garlic plus onions in olive oil in a skillet for 3 minutes over medium heat. Add the remaining ingredients, stirring constantly and scraping the bottom to prevent sticking.
2. Take a nonstick round baking dish and place the mixture inside. Put a sheet of aluminum foil on top.
3. Detach the rotating blade of the air fryer basket. Transfer the baking dish to the air fryer and bake at 204ºC for 20 minutes. When ready, plate up and serve immediately.

Nutrition: Calories: 200kcal, Carbs: 31g, Fat: 3g, Protein: 13g

83. Zucchini and Potato Bowl

Preparation Time: 10 minutes

Cooking time: 45 minutes

Servings: 4

Ingredients:

- 2 potatoes, peeled and cubed
- 4 carrots, cut into chunks
- 1 head broccoli, cut into florets
- 4 zucchinis, sliced thickly
- Salt and ground black pepper, to taste
- 50ml olive oil
- 15g dry onion powder

Directions:

1. In a nonstick round baking dish, add all the ingredients and combine well. Detach the rotating blade of the air fryer basket. Arrange the baking dish in the air fryer.
2. Bake at 204ºC for 45 minutes in the air fryer, ensuring the vegetables are soft and the sides have browned before serving.

Nutrition: Calories: 200kcal, Carbs: 6g, Fat: 17g, Protein: 5g

84. Ravioli

Preparation Time: 10 minutes

Cooking time: 6 minutes

Servings: 4

Ingredients:

- 100 g panko bread crumbs
- 8.4g nutritional yeast
- 5g dried basil
- 5g dried oregano
- 5g garlic powder
- Salt and ground black pepper, to taste
- 50 g aquafaba
- 250 g ravioli
- Cooking spray

Directions:

1. Cover the air fryer basket using aluminum foil and coat with a light brushing of oil.
2. Combine the panko bread crumbs, nutritional yeast, basil, oregano, and garlic powder. Sprinkle with salt and pepper to taste.
3. Put the aquafaba in a separate bowl. Dip the ravioli in the aquafaba before coating it in the panko mixture.
4. Spritz with cooking spray and transfer to the air fryer. Air Fry at 204ºC for 6 minutes. Serve hot.

Nutrition: Calories: 102kcal, Carbs: 14g, Fat: 3g, Protein: 4g

85. Cheesy and Creamy Spinach

Preparation Time: 10 minutes

Cooking time: 15 minutes

Servings: 4

Ingredients:

- 300 g package frozen spinach, thawed and squeezed dry
- 125 g chopped onion
- 2 cloves garlic, minced
- 125 g cream cheese, diced
- 2.84g ground nutmeg
- 5g kosher salt
- 5g black pepper
- 100 g grated Parmesan cheese
- Vegetable oil spray

Directions:

1. Spray a nonstick round baking pan with vegetable oil spray. Combine the spinach, onion, garlic, cream cheese, nutmeg, salt, and pepper in a medium bowl. Transfer to the prepared pan.
2. Detach the rotating blade of the air fryer basket. Put the pan in the air fryer basket.
3. Air Fry at 176 degree C for 10 minutes. Open and stir to thoroughly combine the cream cheese and spinach.
4. Sprinkle the Parmesan cheese on top. Bake within 5 minutes, or until the cheese has melted and browned. Serve hot.

Nutrition: Calories: 230kcal, Carbs: 8g, Fat: 19g, Protein: 13g

86. Cauliflower Roast

Preparation Time: 15 minutes

Cooking time: 20 minutes

Servings: 4

Ingredients:

Cauliflower:

- 1 kg cauliflower florets
- 42.52ml vegetable oil
- 2.84g ground cumin
- 2.84g ground coriander

- 2.84g kosher salt

Sauce:

- 100g Greek yogurt or sour cream
- 50g chopped fresh cilantro
- 1 jalapeño, coarsely chopped
- 4 cloves garlic, peeled
- 2.84g kosher salt
- 28.3g water

Directions:

1. Combine the cauliflower, oil, cumin, coriander, and salt in a large bowl. Toss to coat. Put the cauliflower in the air fryer basket. Air Fry at 204ºC for 20 minutes.

2. Meanwhile, in a blender, combine the yogurt, cilantro, jalapeño, garlic, and salt. Blend, adding the water as needed to keep the blades moving and to thin the sauce.

3. At the end of roasting time, transfer the cauliflower to a large serving bowl. Pour your sauce over then toss gently to coat. Serve immediately.

Nutrition: Calories: 59kcal, Carbs: 3g, Fat: 4g, Protein: 2g

87. Herbed Cheesy Broccoli

Preparation Time: 5 minutes

Cooking time: 18 minutes

Servings: 4

Ingredients:

- 1 large-sized head broccoli, stemmed and cut into small florets
- 40ml canola oil
- 8.4g dried basil
- 8.4g dried rosemary
- Salt and ground black pepper, to taste
- 80g grated yellow cheese

Directions:

1. Bring a pot of lightly salted water to a boil. Put the broccoli florets to the boiling water then let boil for about 3 minutes.

2. Drain the broccoli florets well and transfer them to a large bowl. Add the canola oil, basil, rosemary, salt, and black pepper to the bowl and toss until the broccoli is fully coated.

3. Put the broccoli in your air fryer basket and Air Fry at 199ºC for about 15 minutes or until the broccoli is crisp. Serve the broccoli warm with grated cheese sprinkled on top.

Nutrition: Calories: 27kcal, Carbs: 5g, Fat: 0g, Protein: 3g

88. Cashew Cauliflower

Preparation Time: 5 minutes

Cooking time: 12 minutes

Servings: 2

Ingredients:

- 1 kg cauliflower florets (about half a large head)
- 15ml olive oil
- 5g curry powder
- Salt, to taste
- 100 g toasted, chopped cashews, for garnish

Yogurt Sauce:

- 50 g plain yogurt
- 28.3g sour cream
- 5g honey
- 5g lemon juice
- Pinch cayenne pepper
- Salt, to taste
- 15g fresh cilantro, chopped, + leaves for garnish

Directions:

1. In a large mixing bowl, toss the cauliflower florets with olive oil, curry powder, and salt.
2. Place the cauliflower florets in the air fryer basket and Air Fry at 204ºC for 12 minutes, or until the cauliflower is golden brown.
3. Meanwhile, mix all the fixings for the yogurt sauce in a small bowl and whisk to combine.
4. Remove the cauliflower from the basket and drizzle with the yogurt sauce. Scatter the toasted cashews and cilantro on top and serve immediately.

Nutrition: Calories: 140kcal, Carbs: 14g, Fat: 8g, Protein: 5g

89. Roasted Vegetable Mélange

Preparation Time: 10 minutes

Cooking time: 14-18 minutes

Servings: 4

Ingredients:

- 1 (230 g) package sliced mushrooms
- 1 yellow summer squash, sliced
- 1 red bell pepper, sliced

- 3 cloves garlic, sliced
- 15ml olive oil
- 2.84g dried basil
- 2.84g dried thyme
- 2.84g dried tarragon

Directions:

1. Toss the mushrooms, squash, and bell pepper with the garlic and olive oil in a large bowl until well coated. Mix in the basil, thyme, and tarragon and toss again.
2. Spread the vegetables evenly in the air fryer basket and Air Fry at 176 degree C for 14 to 18 minutes, or until the vegetables are fork-tender. Cool for 5 minutes before serving.

Nutrition: Calories: 80kcal, Carbs: 10g, Fat: 4g, Protein: 1g

90. Sesame Carrots

Preparation Time: 5 minutes

Cooking time: 16 minutes

Servings: 4-6

Ingredients:

- 450 g baby carrots
- 15ml sesame oil
- 2.84g dried dill
- Pinch salt
- Freshly ground black pepper, to taste
- 6 cloves garlic, peeled
- 42.52g sesame seeds

Directions:

1. In a medium bowl, drizzle the baby carrots with the sesame oil. Sprinkle with the dill, salt, and pepper and toss to coat well.
2. Place the baby carrots in the air fryer basket and Air Fry at 193ºC for 8 minutes. Remove the basket and stir in the garlic.
3. Return the basket to the air fryer and roast for another 8 minutes, or until the carrots are lightly browned. Serve sprinkled with the sesame seeds.

Nutrition: Calories: 33kcal, Carbs: 8g, Fat: 2g, Protein: 1g

91. Roasted Brussels Sprouts

Preparation Time: 10 minutes

Cooking time: 20 minutes

Servings: 4

Ingredients:

- 450g fresh Brussels sprouts, trimmed
- 15ml olive oil
- 2.84g salt
- 1/8 teaspoon pepper
- 50g grated Parmesan cheese

Directions:

1. Combine the Brussels sprouts with olive oil, salt, and pepper in a large bowl, and toss until evenly coated.
2. Spread the Brussels sprouts evenly in the air fryer basket and Air Fry at 166ºC for 20 minutes until golden brown and crisp.
3. Sprinkle using the grated Parmesan cheese on top and serve warm.

Nutrition: Calories: 38kcal, Carbs: 8g, Fat: 0g, Protein: 3g

92. Roasted Bell Peppers

Preparation Time: 10 minutes

Cooking time: 22 minutes

Servings: 4

Ingredients:

- 1 green bell pepper, sliced into 1-inch strips
- 1 red bell pepper, sliced into 1-inch strips
- 1 orange bell pepper, sliced into 1-inch strips
- 1 yellow bell pepper, sliced into 1-inch strips
- 28.3ml olive oil, divided
- 2.84g dried marjoram
- Pinch salt
- Freshly ground black pepper, to taste
- 1 head garlic

Directions:

1. Toss the bell peppers with 15ml of olive oil in a large bowl until well coated. Season with marjoram, salt, and pepper. Toss again and set aside.
2. Cut off the top of a head of garlic. Place the garlic cloves on a large square of aluminum foil. Drizzle the top with the remaining 15g of olive oil and wrap the garlic cloves in foil.
3. Transfer the garlic to the air fryer basket and Air Fry at 166ºC for 15 minutes. Add the bell peppers. Air Fry for an additional 7 minutes, or until the garlic is soft and the bell peppers are tender.
4. Transfer the cooked bell peppers to a plate. Remove the garlic and unwrap the foil. Let the garlic rest within a few minutes.
5. Once cooled, squeeze the roasted garlic cloves out of their skins and add them to the plate of bell peppers. Stir well and serve immediately.

Nutrition: Calories: 10kcal, Carbs: 2g, Fat: 0g, Protein: 0g

93. Roasted Mushrooms and Peas

Preparation Time: 5 minutes

Cooking time: 12 minutes

Servings: 4

Ingredients:

- 8.4g melted butter
- 250 g chopped mushrooms
- 250 g cooked rice
- 250 g peas
- 1 carrot, chopped
- 1 red onion, chopped
- 1 garlic clove, minced

- Salt and black pepper, to taste
- 2 hard-boiled eggs, grated
- 15g soy sauce

Directions:

1. Coat a nonstick round baking dish with melted butter. Stir together the mushrooms, cooked rice, peas, carrot, onion, garlic, salt, and pepper in a large bowl until well mixed.
2. Detach the rotating blade of the air fryer basket. Pour the mixture into the prepared baking dish and transfer it to the air fryer basket.
3. Bake at 193ºC for 12 minutes until the vegetables are tender. Divide the mixture among four plates. Serve warm with a sprinkle of grated eggs and a drizzle of soy sauce.

Nutrition: Calories: 50kcal Carbs: 10g, Fat: 2g, Protein: 3g

94. Golden Eggplant Slices

Preparation Time: 5 minutes

Cooking time: 10-12 minutes

Servings: 4

Ingredients:

- 250 g flour
- 4 eggs
- Salt, to taste
- 500 g bread crumbs
- 5g Italian seasoning
- 2 eggplants, sliced
- 2 garlic cloves, sliced
- 28.3g chopped parsley
- Cooking spray

Directions:

1. Oil the air fryer basket with cooking spray. On a plate, place the flour. Whisk the eggs with salt in a shallow bowl. Combine the bread crumbs and Italian seasoning in another shallow bowl.
2. Dredge the eggplant slices, one at a time, in the flour, then in the whisked eggs, finally in the bread crumb mixture to coat well.
3. Arrange the coated eggplant slices in the air fryer basket and Air Fry at 199ºC for 10 to 12 minutes until golden brown and crispy.
4. Transfer your eggplant slices to your plate and sprinkle the garlic and parsley on top before serving.

Nutrition: Calories: 248kcal, Carbs: 26g, Fat: 14g, Protein: 10g

95. Root Vegetable Medley

Preparation Time: 10 minutes

Cooking time: 22 minutes

Servings: 4

Ingredients:

- 2 carrots, sliced
- 2 potatoes, cut into chunks
- 1 rutabaga, cut into chunks
- 1 turnip, cut into chunks
- 1 beet, cut into chunks
- 8 shallots, halved
- 28.3ml olive oil
- Salt and black pepper, to taste
- 28.3g tomato pesto
- 28.3g water
- 28.3g chopped fresh thyme

Directions:

1. Toss the carrots, potatoes, rutabaga, turnip, beet, shallots, olive oil, salt, and pepper in a large mixing bowl until the root vegetables are evenly coated.
2. Place the root vegetables in the air fryer basket and Air Fry at 204ºC for 12 minutes.
3. Meanwhile, in a small bowl, whisk together the tomato pesto and water until smooth.
4. When ready, remove the root vegetables from the basket to a platter. Drizzle with the tomato pesto mixture and sprinkle with thyme. Serve immediately.

Nutrition: Calories: 90kcal, Carbs: 14g, Fat: 3g, Protein: 4g

96. Fried Okra with Chili

Preparation Time: 5 minutes

Cooking time: 10 minutes

Servings: 4

Ingredients:

- 42.52g sour cream
- 28.3g flour
- 28.3g semolina
- 2.84g red chili powder
- Salt and black pepper, to taste

- 450 g okra, halved
- Cooking spray

Directions:

1. Oiled the air fryer basket with cooking spray. In a shallow bowl, place the sour cream. In another shallow bowl, thoroughly combine the flour, semolina, red chili powder, salt, and pepper.

2. Dredge the okra in the sour cream, then roll in the flour mixture until evenly coated.

3. Arrange the okra in the air fryer basket and Air Fry at 204ºC for 10 minutes or until golden brown and crispy. Cool for 5 minutes before serving.

Nutrition: Calories: 120kcal, Carbs: 26g, Fat: 1g, Protein: 3g

97. Panko-Crusted Green Beans

Preparation Time: 5 minutes

Cooking time: 15 minutes

Servings: 4

Ingredients:

- 100 g flour
- 2 eggs
- 250 g panko bread crumbs
- 100 g grated Parmesan cheese
- 5g cayenne pepper
- Salt and black pepper, to taste
- 700 g green beans

Directions:

1. In a bowl, place the flour. In a separate bowl, lightly beat the eggs. In a separate shallow bowl, thoroughly combine the bread crumbs, cheese, cayenne pepper, salt, and pepper.

2. Dip the green beans in the flour, then in the beaten eggs, finally in the bread crumb mixture to coat well.

3. Place the green beans in the air fryer basket and Air Fry at 204ºC for 15 minutes or until they are cooked to the desired crispiness. Remove from the basket to a bowl and serve.

Nutrition: Calories: 100kcal, Carbs: 13g, Fat: 2g, Protein: 10g

98. Halloumi Zucchinis and Eggplant

Preparation Time: 5 minutes

Cooking time: 14 minutes

Servings: 2

Ingredients:

- 2 zucchinis, cut into even chunks
- 1 large eggplant, peeled, cut into chunks
- 1 large carrot, cut into chunks
- 175 g halloumi cheese, cubed
- 8.4ml olive oil
- Salt and black pepper, to taste
- 5g dried mixed herbs

Directions:

1. Combine the zucchinis, eggplant, carrot, cheese, olive oil, salt, and pepper in a large bowl and toss to coat well.
2. Spread the mixture evenly in the air fryer basket and Air Fry at 171ºC for 14 minutes until crispy and golden. Serve topped with mixed herbs.

Nutrition: Calories: 68kcal, Carbs: 4g, Fat: 5g, Protein: 2g

99. Fajita Meatball Wraps with Lettuce

Preparation Time: 10 minutes

Cooking time: 10 minutes

Servings: 4

Ingredients:

- 450 g 85% lean ground beef
- 100 g salsa, plus more for serving
- 50 g chopped onions
- 50 g diced green or red bell peppers
- 1 large egg, beaten
- 5g fine sea salt
- 2.84g chili powder
- 2.84g ground cumin
- 1 clove garlic, minced
- Cooking spray

For Serving:

- 8 leaves Boston lettuce
- Pico de Gallo or salsa
- Lime slices

Directions:

1. Oiled the air fryer basket with cooking spray. In a large bowl, mix together all the ingredients until well combined.
2. Shape the meat mixture into eight 1-inch balls. Place the meatballs in the air fryer basket, leaving a little space between them.
3. Air fry at 176 degree C for 10 minutes, or until cooked through and no longer pink inside and the internal temperature reaches 63ºC.
4. Serve each meatball on a lettuce leaf, topped with Pico de Gallo or salsa. Serve with lime slices.

Nutrition: Calories: 342kcal, Carbs: 11g, Fat: 12g, Protein: 47g

100. Vegan Nugget and Veggie Taco

Preparation Time: 5 minutes

Cooking time: 15 minutes

Servings: 4

Ingredients:

- 15ml water
- 4 pieces commercial vegan nuggets, chopped
- 1 small yellow onion, diced
- 1 small red bell pepper, chopped
- 2 cobs grilled corn kernels
- 4 large corn tortillas
- Mixed greens, for garnish

Directions:

1. Over medium heat, sauté the nuggets in the water with the onion, corn kernels and bell pepper in a skillet, then remove from the heat.
2. Fill the tortillas with the nuggets plus vegetables then fold them up. Transfer to the inside of the fryer and air fry at 204ºC for 15 minutes.
3. Once crispy, serve immediately, garnished with the mixed greens.

Nutrition: Calories: 281kcal, Carbs: 30g, Fat: 11g, Protein: 16g

CHAPTER 6: Desserts

101. Pistachio Brownies

Preparation Time: 10 minutes

Cooking time: 20 minutes

Servings: 4

Ingredients:

- 75ml milk
- 2.84g vanilla extract
- 25g salt
- 25g pecans
- 75g flour
- 75g sugar
- 25g cocoa powder
- 15g ground flax seeds

Directions:

1. Combine all the dry fixings in your bowl. Mix the wet fixings in your second bowl. Mix both mixtures until well blended.
2. Preheat the air fryer to 175ºC. Line a 5-inch cake tin with parchment paper and pour the brownie mixture. Put it in your basket, and cook within 20 minutes. Serve!

Nutrition: Calories: 486kcal; Carbs: 25g; Fat: 26g; Protein: 25g

102. Lemon Pies

Preparation Time: 10 minutes

Cooking time: 10 minutes

Servings: 6

Ingredients:

- 1 pack of pastry, cut out into 6 circles
- 1 egg beaten
- 200g lemon curd
- 225g powdered sugar
- Half of lemon

Directions:

1. Preheat the air fryer to 180ºC.
2. Add 15g of lemon curd to each pastry circle, brush the sides with egg, and fold.
3. Press around the sides using your fork to secure. Brush the pies with egg, put it in your basket, and cook within10 minutes.
4. Mix the lemon juice with the powdered sugar to make the icing and drizzle on the cooked pies. Serve and enjoy!

Nutrition: Calories: 646kcal; Carbs: 45g; Fat: 26g; Protein: 25g

103. Apple Fritters

Preparation Time: 15 minutes

Cooking time: 15 minutes

Servings: 4

Ingredients:

- 225g self-rising flour
- 200g Greek yoghurt
- 8.4g sugar
- 15g cinnamon
- 1 apple peeled and chopped
- 225g icing sugar
- 28.3ml milk
- Cooking spray

Directions:

1. Mix the flour, yoghurt, sugar, cinnamon, and apple in a bowl. Knead for about 3 -4 minutes, divide into four and flatten it.
2. Meanwhile, blend the icing sugar and milk in your small bowl and keep it aside.
3. Prepare your air fryer basket using parchment paper, then grease using the cooking spray.
4. Cook the apple fritters in your air fryer for 15 minutes at 185ºC. Drizzle with glaze and serve!

Nutrition: Calories: 305kcal; Carbs: 66g; Fat: 1g; Protein: 9g

104. Chocolate Shortbread Balls

Preparation Time: 10 minutes

Cooking time: 14 minutes

Servings: 9 balls

Ingredients:
- 175g butter
- 75g caster sugar
- 250g plain flour
- 8.4g vanilla essence
- 9 chocolate chunks
- 28.3g cocoa powder

Directions:
1. Warm your air fryer to 180ºC.
2. Combine the flour, sugar, cocoa butter, and vanilla in your bowl, then knead the mixture into a smooth dough.
3. Divide the mixture into 9, place a chunk of chocolate in each piece, and form into balls, covering the chocolate.
4. Cook the chocolate shortbread balls in your air fryer for 8 minutes at 180ºC. Toss the chocolate shortbread and cook for 6 minutes at 160ºC. Serve and enjoy!

Nutrition: Calories: 282kcal; Carbs: 30g; Fat: 16g; Protein: 3g

105. Apple Blackberry Crumble

Preparation Time: 5 minutes

Cooking time: 15 minutes

Servings: 4

Ingredients:

- 4 diced apples
- 150g frozen blackberries
- 50g brown rice flour
- 56g sugar
- 5g cinnamon
- 56g butter

Directions:

1. Preheat the air fryer to 150ºC.
2. Mix the apple and blackberries in an air fryer-safe baking pan.
3. Mix the flour, sugar, cinnamon, and butter in a bowl, then spoon it over the apple and blackberry.
4. Cook the apple blackberry crumble in your air fryer for 15 minutes. Serve and enjoy!

Nutrition: Calories: 310kcal; Carbs: 50g; Fat - 12g; Protein - 2g

106. Cherry Pies

Preparation Time: 10 minutes

Cooking time: 10 minutes

Servings: 6

Ingredients:

- 300g prepared short crust pastry, cut into 6 pies
- 75g cherry pie filling
- Cooking spray
- 42g icing sugar
- 2.84ml milk

Directions:

1. Add 1 7g cherry pie filling to each pie pastry, fold the dough in half and seal around the edges with a fork.
2. Put it in your greased basket, and cook within 10 minutes at 175ºC.
3. Mix the icing sugar and milk, then drizzle it over cooled pies. Serve and enjoy!

Nutrition: Calories: 686kcal; Carbs: 28g; Fat: 27g; Protein: 21g

107. Lemon Tarts

Preparation Time: 10 minutes

Cooking time: 15 minutes

Servings: 8

Ingredients:

- 100g butter
- 225g plain flour
- 30g caster sugar
- Zest and juice of 1 lemon
- 4 tsp lemon curd

Directions:

1. Mix the butter, flour, and sugar in a bowl until it forms crumbs, then add the lemon zest and juice.
2. Add a little water at a time until you have a dough. Roll out the dough and line 8 small ramekins with it.
3. Add 1.42g of lemon curd to each ramekin and cook in the air fryer for 15 minutes at 180ºC. Serve and enjoy!

Nutrition: Calories: 318kcal; Carbs: 27g; Fat: 10g; Protein: 3g

108. Chocolate-Dipped Balls

Preparation Time: 15 minutes

Cooking time: 15 minutes

Servings: 6

Ingredients:

- 225g self-rising flour
- 100g sugar
- 100g butter
- 50ml milk chocolate, melted
- 1 egg beaten
- 5g vanilla essence

Directions:

1. Mix the flour, butter, and sugar in a bowl. Mix in the egg plus vanilla to form a dough. Split the dough into 6 and form it into balls.
2. Put it in your basket and cook within 15 minutes at 180ºC. Dip the cooked biscuits into the chocolate and serve!

Nutrition: Calories: 374kcal; Carbs: 49g; Fat: 17g; Protein: 5g

109. Fruit Scones

Preparation Time: 10 minutes

Cooking time: 8 minutes

Servings: 2

Ingredients:

- 225g self-rising flour
- 50g butter
- 50g sultanas
- 25g caster sugar
- 1 egg
- A little milk

Directions:

1. Combine the flour plus butter in your bowl. Add the sultanas and mix them well. Stir in the caster sugar.

2. Add the egg and mix it well. Add the milk until you have a dough. Shape the dough into scones.

3. Place in the air fryer and cook at 180ºC for 8 minutes. Serve and enjoy!

Nutrition: Calories: 374kcal; Carbs: 57g; Fat: 12g; Protein: 8g

110. Wonton-Wrapped Banana Bites

Preparation Time: 10 minutes

Cooking time: 6 minutes

Servings: 12 bites

Ingredients:

- 1 banana, sliced
- 12 wonton wrappers
- 75g peanut butter
- 1-8.4ml vegetable oil
- Water, as needed
- Juice from 1 lemon

Directions:

1. Mix the lemon juice, and water in a bowl. Add the bananas, and soak it for a while.
2. Place one piece of banana and a spoon of peanut butter in each wonton wrapper. Wet the sides and seal it.
3. Put the wrapped banana in your greased basket, and cook for 6 minutes at 190ºC. Serve!

Nutrition: Calories: 386kcal; Carbs: 20g; Fat: 26g; Protein: 21g

111. Almond Orange Cake

Preparation Time: 15 minutes

Cooking time: 20 minutes

Servings: 6

Ingredients:

- 80 g almonds, chopped

- 42.52g orange marmalade
- 1 stick butter
- 2.84g allspice, ground
- 2.84g anise seed, ground
- 2.84g baking powder
- 5g baking soda
- 175 g almond flour
- 28.3g Truvia for baking
- 2 eggs plus 1 egg yok, beaten
- Olive oil cooking spray for pans

Directions:

1. Lightly grease cake pan with olive oil cooking spray. Mix the butter and Truvia until nice and smooth.
2. Fold in the eggs, almonds, marmalade; beat again until well mixed.   Add flour, baking soda, baking powder, allspice, star anise and ground cinnamon.
3. Bake in the preheated air-fryer at 154 degree C for 20-minutes. Serve.

Nutrition: Calories: 331kcal, Carbs: 47g, Fat: 14g, Protein: 5g

112. Air-Fried Apricots in Whiskey Sauce

Preparation Time: 15 minutes

Cooking time: 35 minutes

Servings: 4

Ingredients:

- 500 g apricot, pitted and halved
- 50 g whiskey
- 5g pure vanilla extract
- ½ stick butter, room temperature
- 100 g maple syrup sugar-free

Directions:

1. Heat-up the maple syrup, vanilla, butter in a small saucepan over medium heat; simmer until the butter is melted.
2. Add the whiskey and stir to combine. Arrange the apricots on the bottom of the lightly greased baking dish.
3. Pour the sauce over the apricots; scatter whole cloves over the top. Then, transfer the baking dish to the pre-heated air-fryer. Air-fry at 193 degree C for 35-minutes.

Nutrition: Calories: 356kcal, Fat: 17g, Carbs: 43.3g, Protein: 38.2g

113. Date & Hazelnut Cookies

Preparation Time: 15 minutes

Cooking time: 20 minutes

Servings: 10

Ingredients:

- 42.52g sugar-free maple syrup
- 80 g dated, dried
- 50 g hazelnuts, chopped
- 1 stick butter, room temperature
- 100 g almond flour
- 100 g cornflour
- 28.3g Truvia for baking
- 2.84g vanilla extract
- 1/3 teaspoon ground cinnamon
- 2.84g cardamom

Directions:

1. Firstly, cream the butter with Truvia and maple syrup until the mixture is fluffy. Sift both types of flour into a bowl with a butter mixture. Add remaining ingredients.
2. Now, knead the mixture to form a dough; place in the fridge for 20-minutes.
3. To finish, shape the chilled dough into bite-size balls; arrange them on a baking dish and flatten balls with the back of a spoon. Bake the cookies for 20-minutes at 154 degree C.

Nutrition: Calories: 187kcal, Fat: 10.5g, Carbs: 23.2g, Protein: 1.5g

114. Coconut Strawberry Fritters

Preparation Time: 5 minutes

Cooking time: 4 minutes

Servings: 8

Ingredients:

- 175 g almond flour
- 2.84g baking powder
- 2.84g coconut extract
- 300 g soy milk
- 1/8 teaspoon salt
- 28.3g Truvia for baking
- 350 g strawberries

- 42.52ml coconut oil

Directions:

1. Thoroughly combine all ingredients in a bowl. Next, drop teaspoon amounts of the mix into the air-fryer cooking basket; air-fry for 4-minutes at 173 degree C. Serve.

Nutrition: Calories: 145kcal, Fat: 6g, Carbs: 20.7g, Protein: 2.8g

115. Festive Baileys Brownie

Preparation Time: 15 minutes

Cooking time: 25 minutes

Servings: 8

Ingredients:

- 75 g Ricotta cheese, room temperature
- 28.3g Truvia for baking
- 100 ml sour cream
- 250 g semisweet chocolate chips
- 28.3g Baileys
- ½ box brownie mix
- Olive oil cooking spray

Directions:

1. In a bowl, mix brownie batter according to package. Add the batter to a lightly greased baking pan. Air-fry for 25-minutes at 179 degree C. Allow cooling on the wire rack.

2. Microwave the chocolate chips until melted. Allow the batter to cool at room temperature. Add the Baileys, sour cream, Truvia and mix until well combined. Spread the mixture on top of your brownie.

Nutrition: Calories: 415kcal, Fat: 19.6g, Carbs: 57.7g, Protein: 22.3g

116. Baked Pears with Chocolate

Preparation Time: 15 minutes

Cooking time: 35 minutes

Servings: 4

Ingredients:

- 4 firm-ripe pears, peeled, cored and sliced
- 28.3g Truvia for baking
- 2.84g ground star anise
- 5g pure vanilla extract
- 5g orange extract
- ½ stick butter, cold

- 100 g chocolate chips for garnish

Directions:

1. Grease the baking dish with olive oil cooking spray; lay pear slices on the bottom of the pan. In a bowl, mix Truvia, star anise, vanilla and orange extract.

2. Sprinkle this mixture over the fruit layer. Cut in the butter and scatter it evenly over the top. Bake at 193 degree C for 35-minutes. Serve sprinkled with chocolate chips for garnish.

Nutrition: Calories: 109kcal, Carbs: 17g, Fat: 5g, Protein: 1g

117. Apricot Jam Dumplings

Preparation Time: 15 minutes

Cooking time: 27 minutes

Servings: 4

Ingredients:

- 4 sheets of puff pastry
- 80 g apricot jam
- 80 g pine nuts, chopped
- 2.84g ginger, grated
- 2.84g ground cinnamon
- 2.84g vanilla extract
- ½ stick butter, melted
- 28.3g Truvia for baking

Directions:

1. In a mixing dish, combine Truvia, cinnamon, pine nuts, vanilla, ginger and apricot jam. Divide the mixture amongst 4 pastry sheets.

2. Fold the pastry sheets over the filling and seal the edges. Brush the dumplings with melted butter. Air-fry at 173 degree C for 27 minutes.

Nutrition: Calories: 50kcal, Carbs: 13g, Fat: 0g, Protein: 0g

118. Cheesy Orange Fritters

Preparation Time: 5 minutes

Cooking time: 4 minutes

Servings: 8

Ingredients:

- 25ml orange juice
- 2.84g ground star anise
- 1/3 teaspoon ground cinnamon

- 28.3g Truvia for baking
- 300 g almond flour
- 5g vanilla extract
- 175ml whole milk
- 5g orange rind, grated
- 350 g cream cheese, at room temperature

Directions:

1. Combine all the ingredients in a bowl. Next, drop teaspoons of the mixture into the air-fryer cooking basket; air-fry for 4-minutes at 171 degree C.

Nutrition: Calories: 268kcal, Fat: 15.8g, Carbs: 25.8g, Protein: 6g

119. Lemon Mini Pies with Coconut

Preparation Time: 5 minutes

Cooking time: 5 minutes

Servings: 8

Ingredients:

- 1 box of lemon instant pudding
- filling mix (4-serving size)
- 2.84g ground star anise
- 1/8 teaspoon salt
- 5g pure vanilla extract
- 300g cream cheese, room temperature
- 80 g coconut, shredded
- 18 wonton wrappers
- 5g lemon peel, grated

Directions:

1. Oil muffin pans with olive oil cooking spray. Press the wonton wrappers evenly into cups. Transfer them into your air fryer and bake for 5-minutes at 176 degree C.

2. When the edges are golden in color, they are ready. Meanwhile, blend all remaining ingredients using a blender. Place the prepared cream in the fridge until ready to serve.

3. Lastly, divide prepared cream among wrappers and keep refrigerated until ready to eat.

Nutrition: Calories: 107kcal, Carbs: 17g, Fat: 4g, Protein: 1g

120. Peach Cake

Preparation Time: 15 minutes

Cooking time: 35 minutes

Servings: 6

Ingredients:

- 250 g peaches, pitted and mashed
- 2.84g baking powder
- 300 g almond flour
- 2.84g orange extract
- 1.42g nutmeg, freshly grated
- 2 eggs
- 28.3g Truvia for baking
- 80 g ghee
- 1.42g ground cinnamon
- 5g pure vanilla extract

Directions:

1. Preheat your air-fryer to 154 degree C. Spritz the cake pan with olive oil cooking spray. In a mixing bowl, beat the ghee with Truvia until creamy.
2. Fold in the egg, mashed peaches and honey. Then, make the cake batter by mixing the remaining ingredients; now, stir in the peach mixture with the rest of the ingredients.
3. Pour batter into cake pan and level the surface of the batter. Bake 35-minutes and enjoy!

Nutrition: Calories: 317kcal, Fat: 13.1g, Carbs: 46.8g, Protein: 4.7g

Conclusion

An air fryer may be used for essentially anything. The air fryer can do it all, from making crispy potato chips to frying eggs and bacon to cooking chicken wings in a matter of minutes. So the air fryer is your new best buddy if you're seeking for quick meals with less oil these days. The air fryer is becoming more popular, with people who want to improve their lifestyle and still enjoy meals that they love. When used correctly, the air fryer can replace many of the unhealthy items you would buy at a fast food restaurant. It is much healthier and thinner than fries or fried foods from the store. Not to mention that there are no bad fats or oils in any of these cooking methods!

It also works great for baked goods because it can bake bread, cakes, cookies, etc. This is a great alternative to an oven or a stove top because it does not use much power and can be used easily around other items in the kitchen. This can be extremely useful if you have a small kitchen and want to continue cooking your favorite meals but want a healthier option. It can also be used on vacation so that you do not need to spend money on high-priced fast food when you reach your destination. You will also feel healthier the next day if you do not eat fast food, which has been scientifically proven.

In the past, the only way to make a healthy meal was to eat protein and vegetables, but now you can eat those foods and enjoy them in a different way. Air fryers are able to use much less oil when cooking than other methods of cooking. You will not need so much oil when frying food in an air fryer as opposed to how much you normally would. It is healthier because there is no used oils as well.

The air fryer has recently become a massive part of many individuals lives, turning simple meals into gourmet ones. It's easy to use, and the food that it produces is delicious. So, if you are looking for a long time for a way to cut down on some of the oil or grease you use when cooking food, the air fryer is your answer.

By following the step-by-step instructions that are designed specifically for you without using complex phrases or often used terms, this cookbook's content will assist you in learning exactly how to accomplish this. We'll show you how to use an air fryer to quickly and conveniently prepare and cook delicious, healthy dishes.

Happy cooking, everyone!

Printed in Great Britain
by Amazon

26460978R00059